Through the Eyes of A Teen

I0390477

Nontraditional photos of California Landmarks

By Riki Smith

Photographs and commentary by Riki Smith
Front cover photograph by K. S. S.
Back cover photograph by R. N. S.

This book is dedicated to Granny, Jiji and Baba, and to the people who feed me.

Table of Contents

Preface

To learn about teenagers, adults usually look at our music choices, social media and YouTube. Although those things will provide a lot of information, they don't tell the whole story. It is very easy for adults to think that the way they see things in the world are seen in the same way by teens. Sometimes this is true, but other times we see shapes, colors and objects differently.

When taking the photos in this book, I was looking for unique ways to do it. I didn't want my photos to look like pictures in a travel magazine. I wanted to show how things relate to their surroundings. I also wanted to show how shadows actually change the way an object looks, and that shapes can look like many different things.

Through the Eyes of A Teen: Nontraditional Photos of California Landmarks is my photo essay of two well known California landmarks, Joshua Tree National Park and Salton Sea, and two landmarks that are not well known, Salvation Mountain and Slab City. Most of the photos were taken using a digital SLR camera. That made it easier for me to show you the things that I saw, and the way that I saw them. The other photos were taken using a smart phone camera, which gave me a chance to take very quick shots when I didn't want to pull out my other camera. I have written some information about each place that I visited and included my personal comments.

The trip lasted 16 hours. We traveled a total of 551 miles (887 km) by car. I actually drove 5 miles (8 km). During the trip, we were as high 5,185 feet (1,580.4 m) above sea level (Key's View in Joshua Tree National Park) and as low as 227 feet (69.19 m) below sea level (Salton Sea).

Joshua Tree National Park

Joshua Tree National Park is located in southeastern California. It was designated a U.S. National Monument in 1936, and declared a U.S. National Park in 1994. The park was named for the Joshua trees, which are native to the area. Joshua Tree National Park covers a land area of 760,626 acres (1,235.37 sq mi; 3,199.59 sq km). The park includes parts of two deserts – the Mojave Desert and the Colorado Desert. The Little San Bernardino Mountains also run through a portion of the park. Joshua Tree contains spectacular rock formations that were formed more than 100 million years ago, stunning vegetation and magnificent deserts.

At first, I thought it was very pointless to go to a national park that was 150 miles (214.4 km) away from where I live. I thought it was just another national park with trees and hiking trails. I didn't think that anything would be exciting if I went there. After visiting Joshua Tree, it was fun because I got to see a very nice view of the Imperial Valley and the rock formations were very interesting. I also liked the fact that it was very quiet and very peaceful.

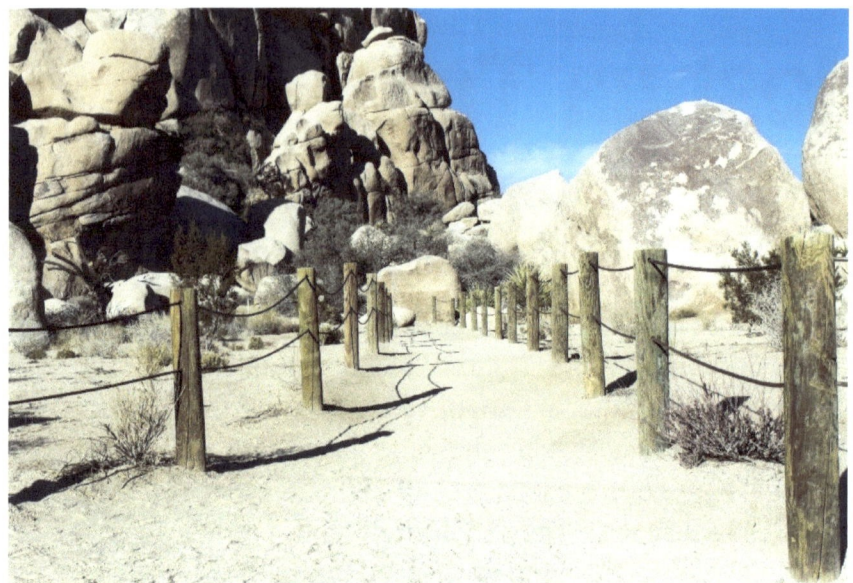

Entrance to Hidden Valley

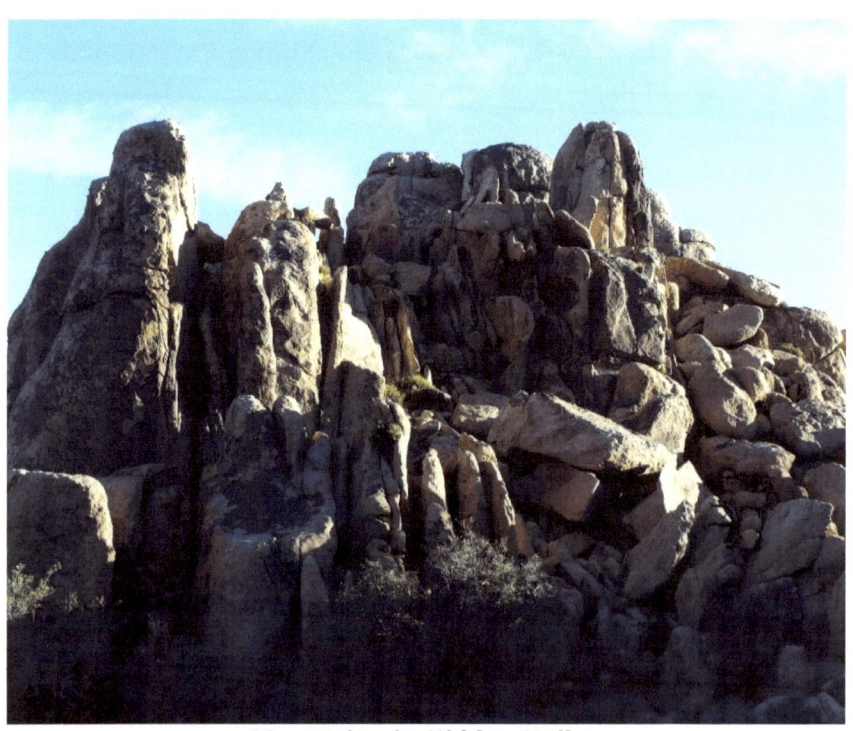

Mountains in Hidden Valley

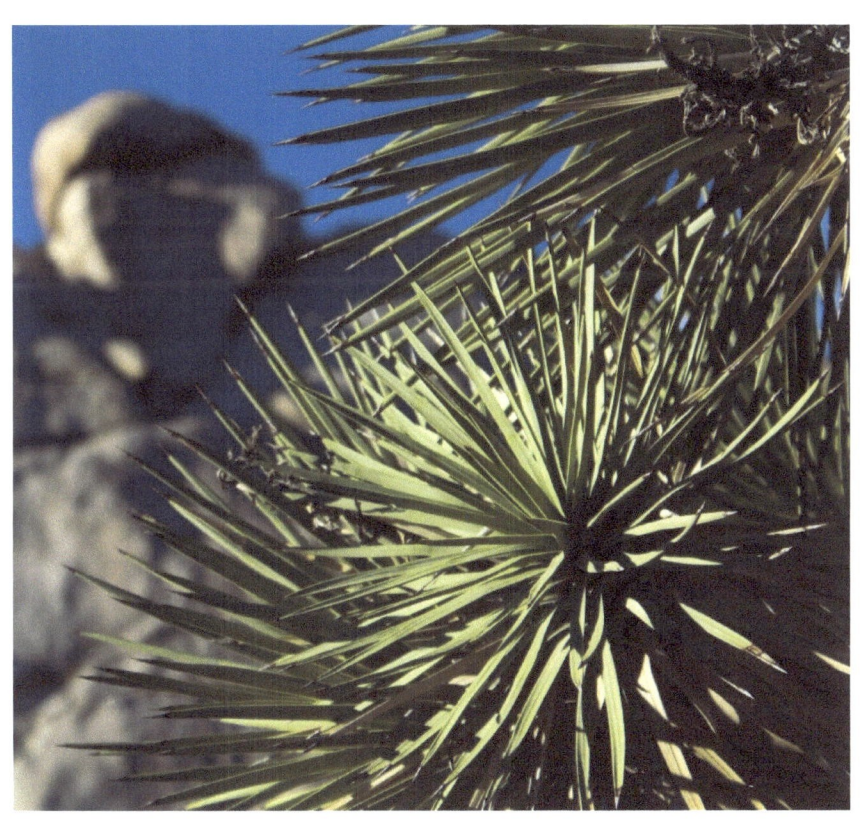

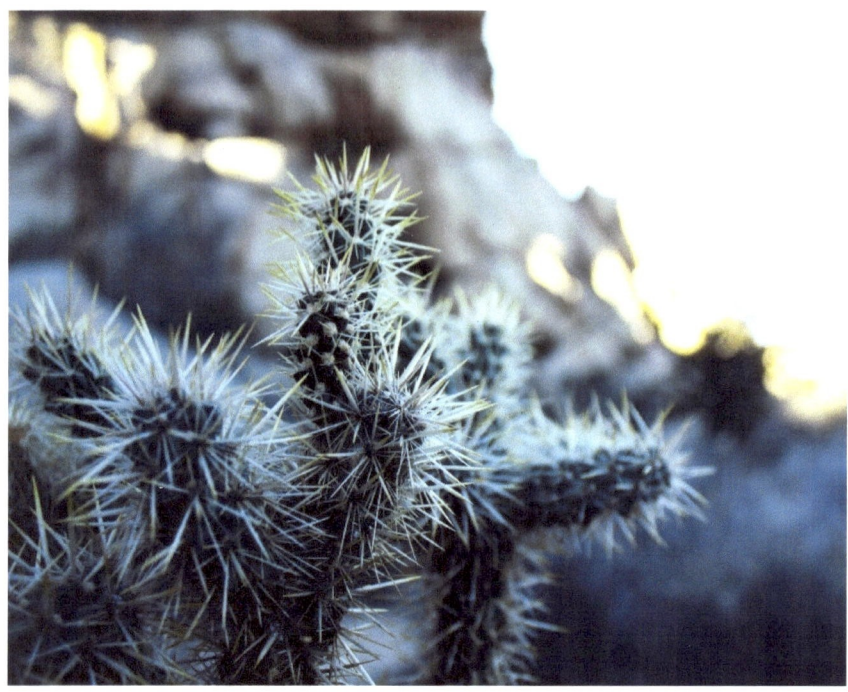

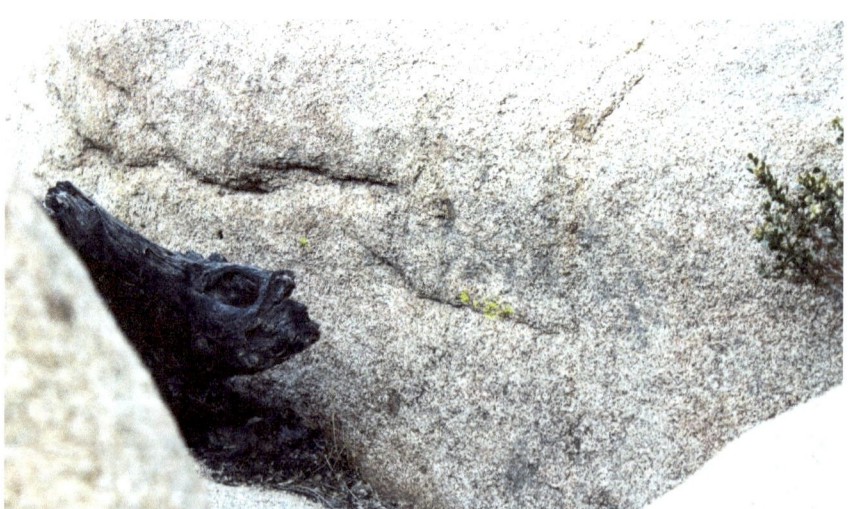

A tree limb that looks like a face

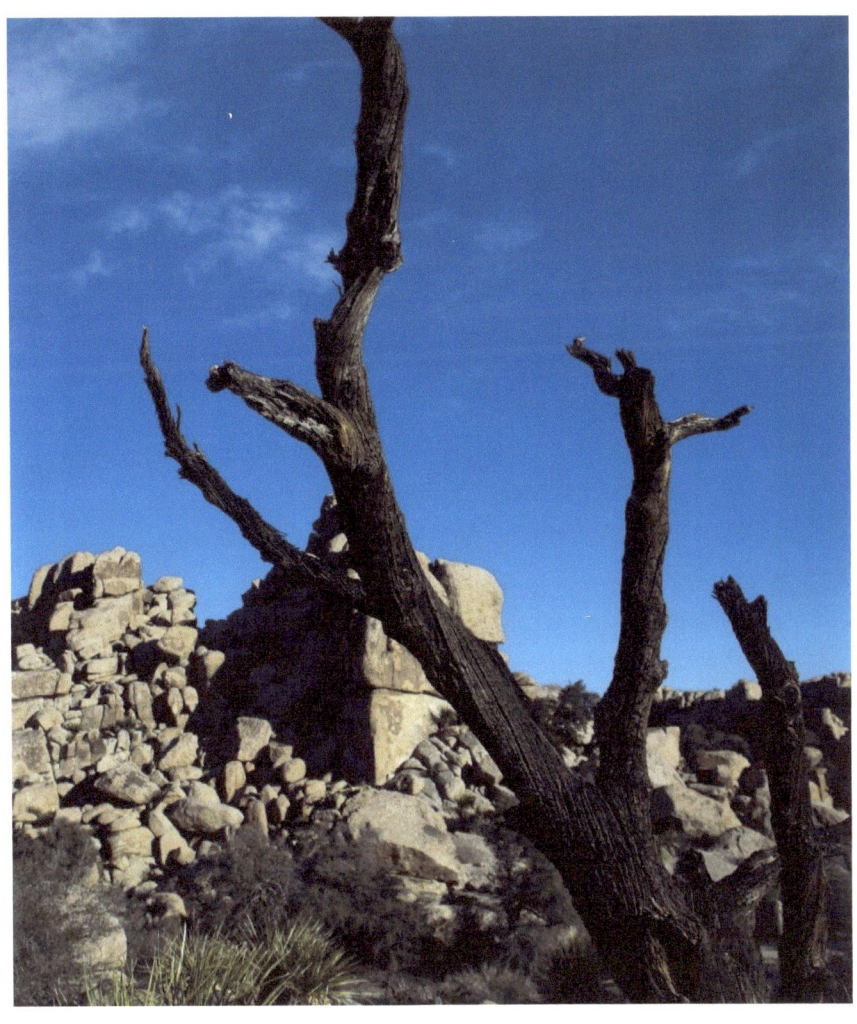

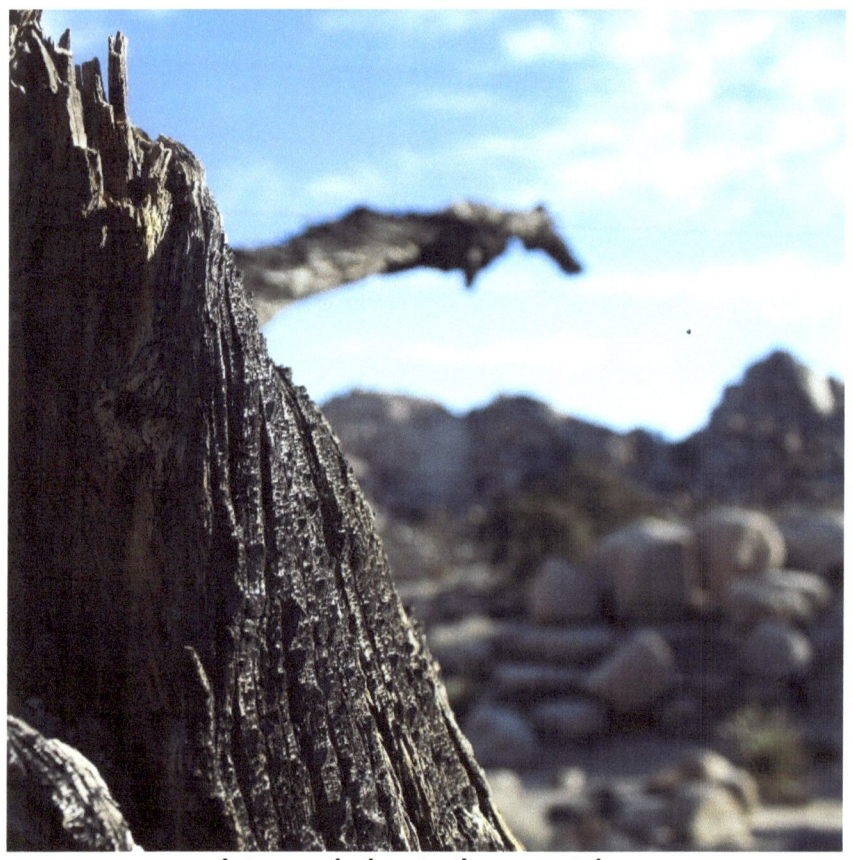

A tree pointing to the mountains

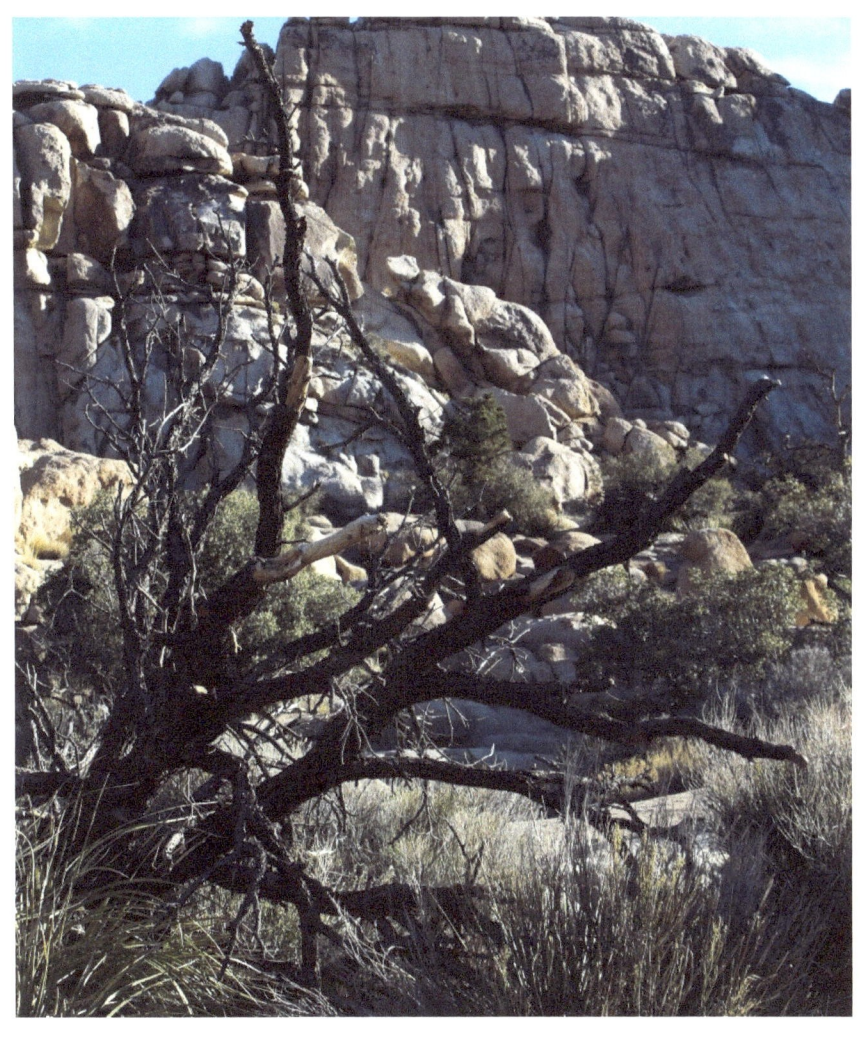

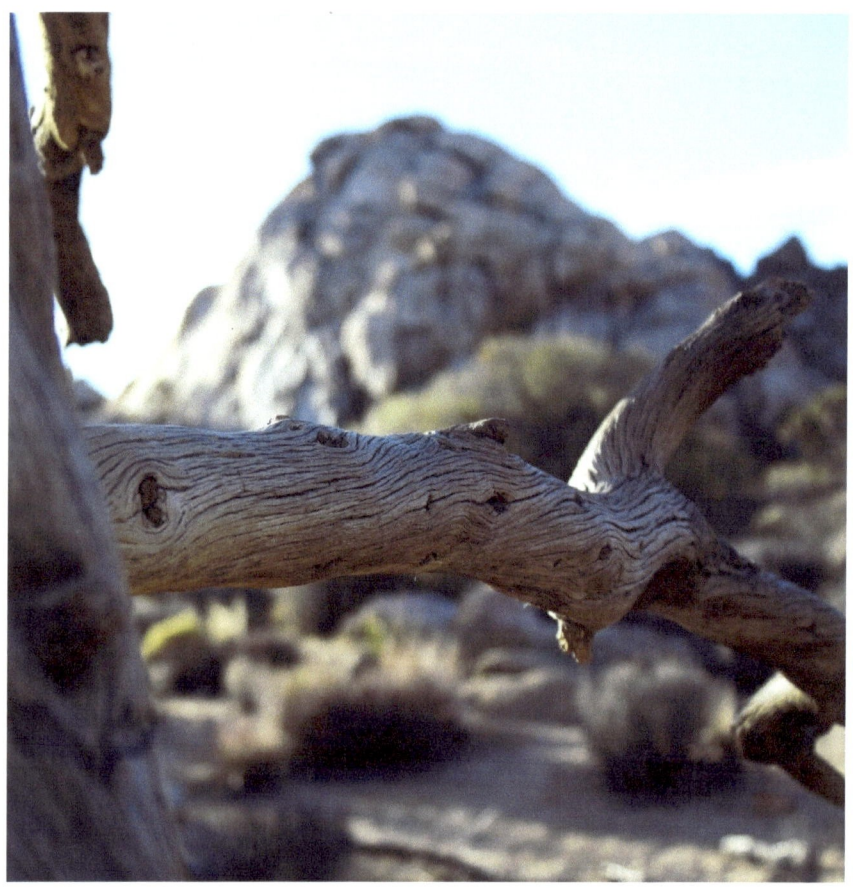

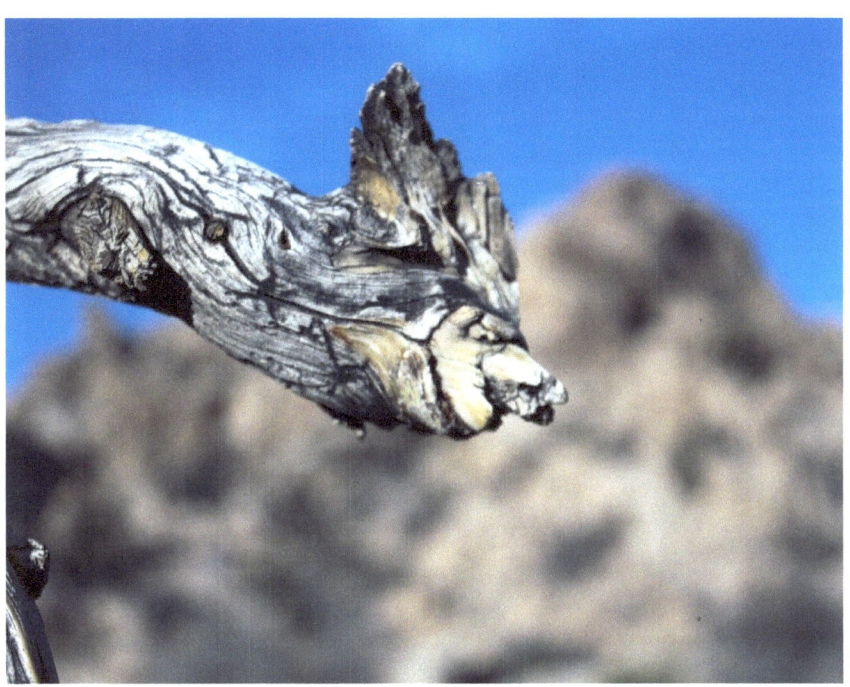

A branch resembling the head of a wolf

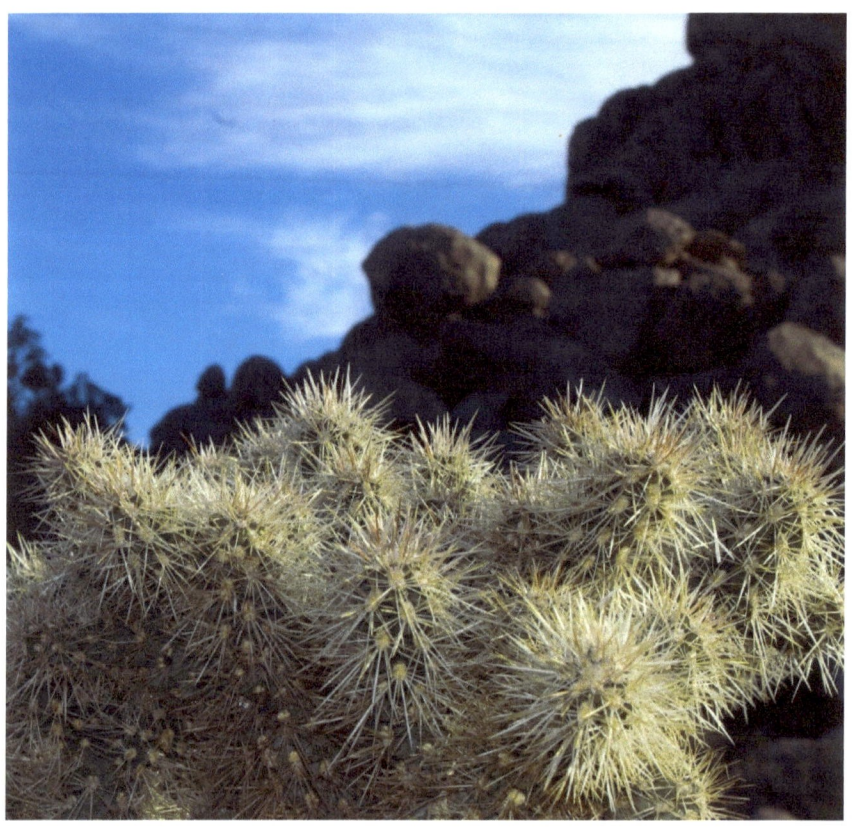

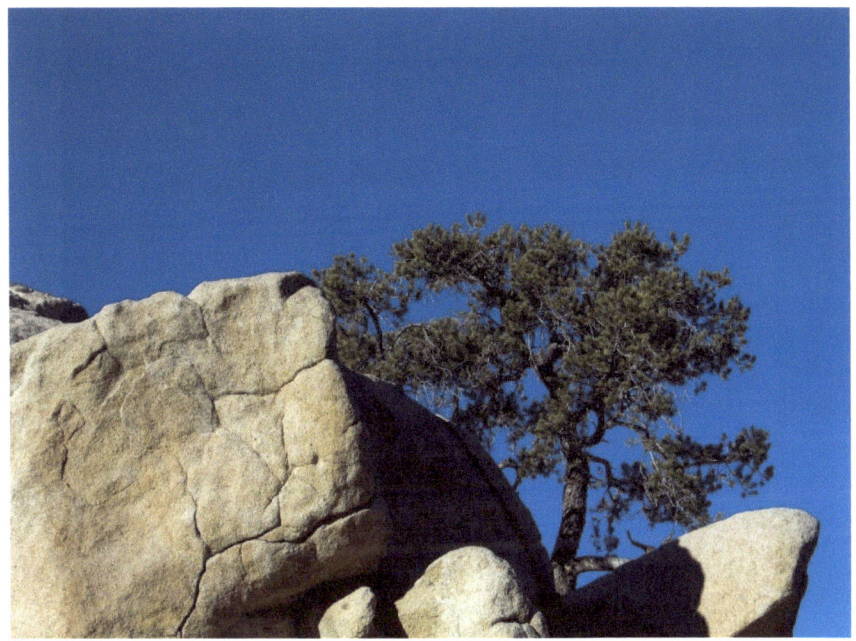

A rock holding out its arms to be hugged

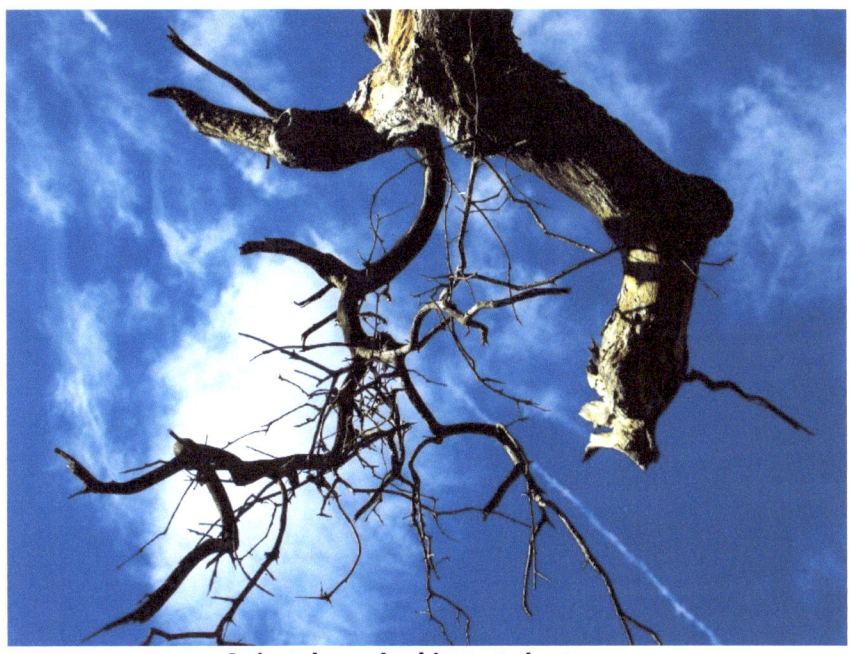

Lying down looking at the trees

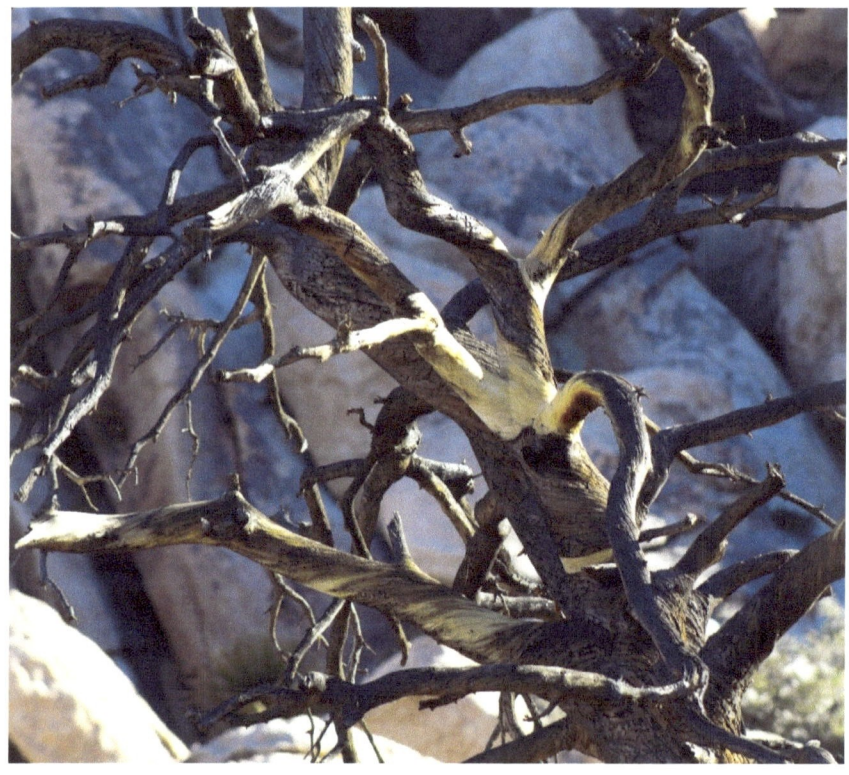

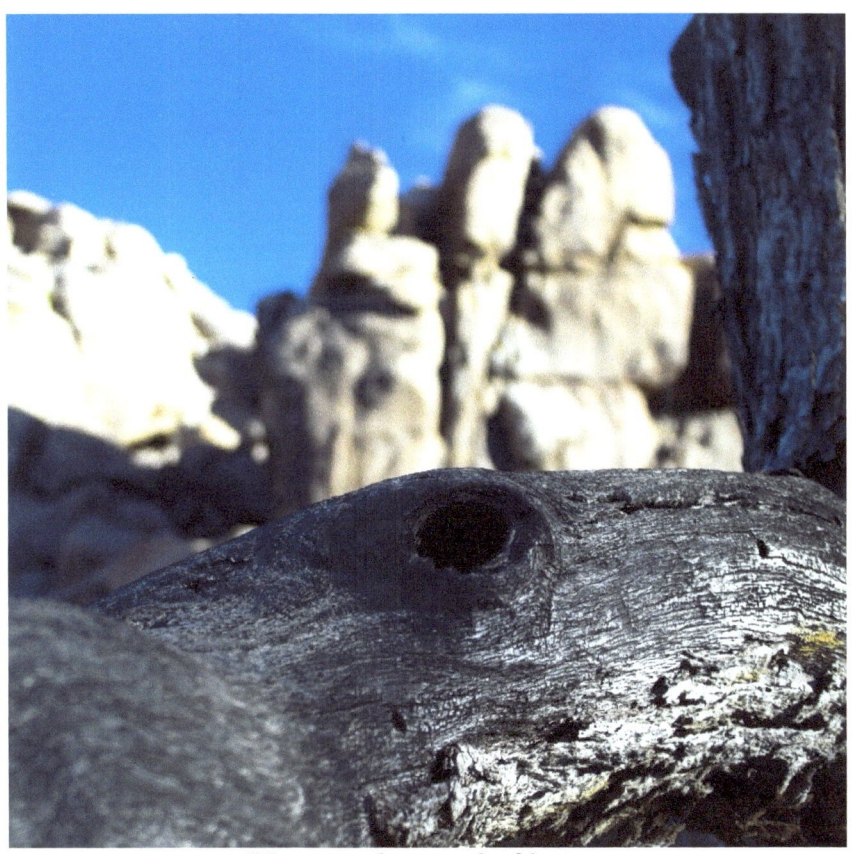

The eye of a tree looking up

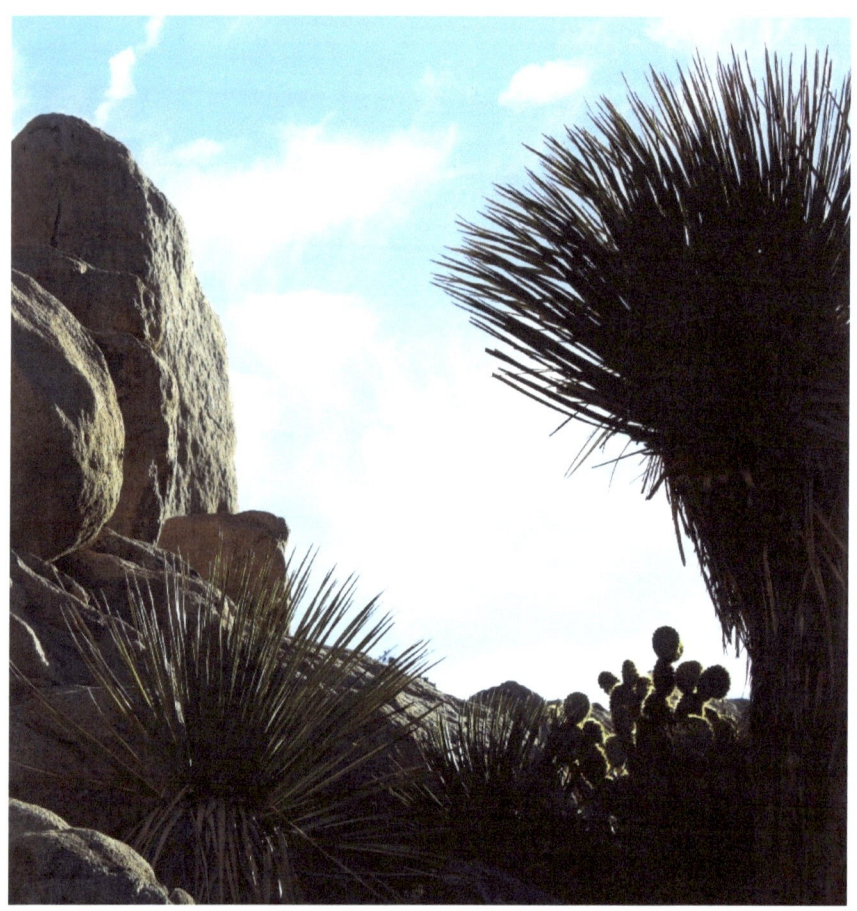

A cactus mountain road

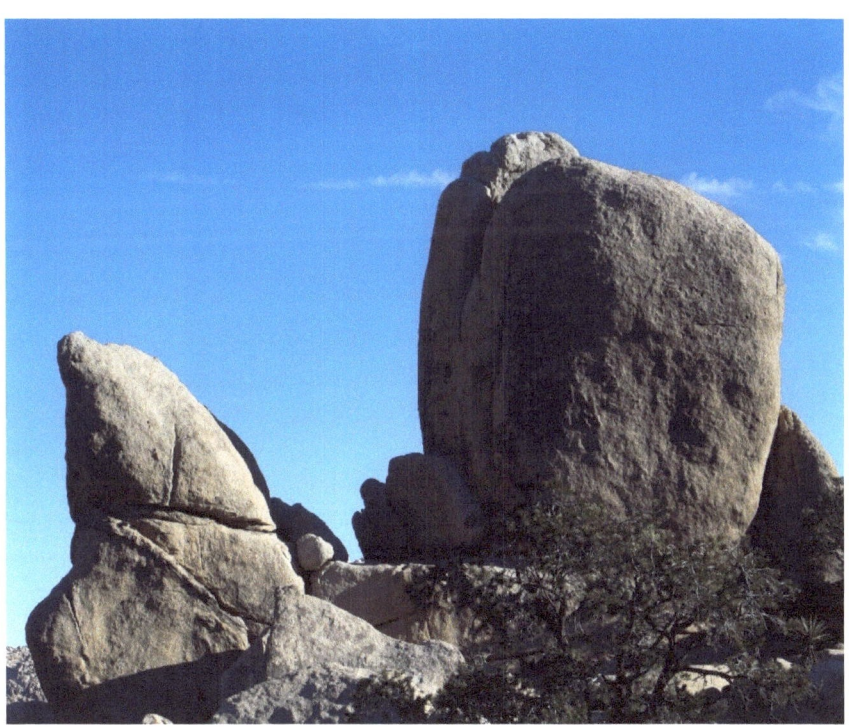

Rocks that look like a snail

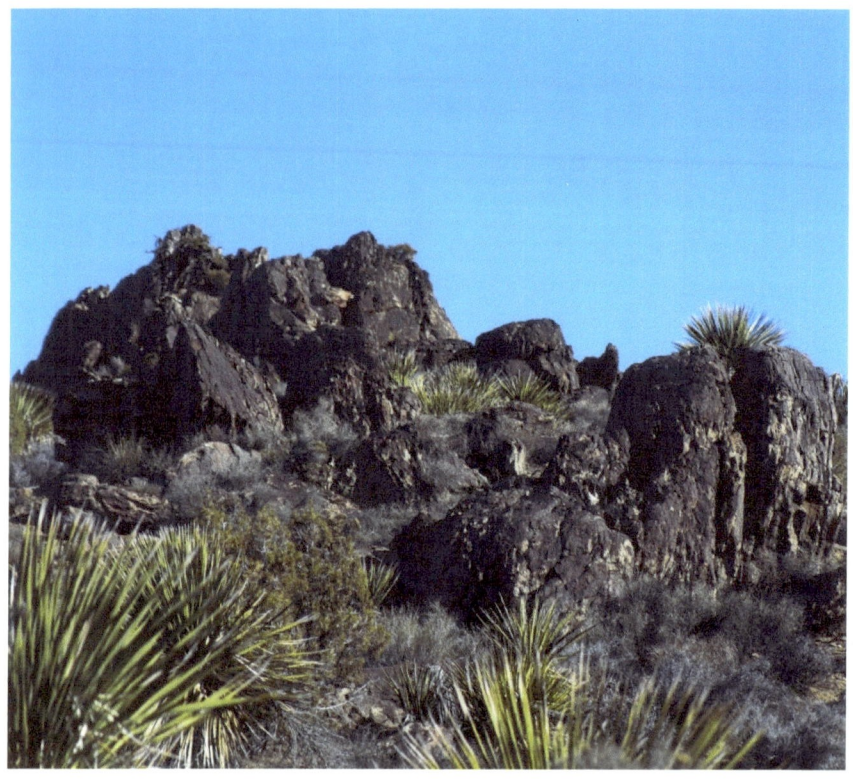

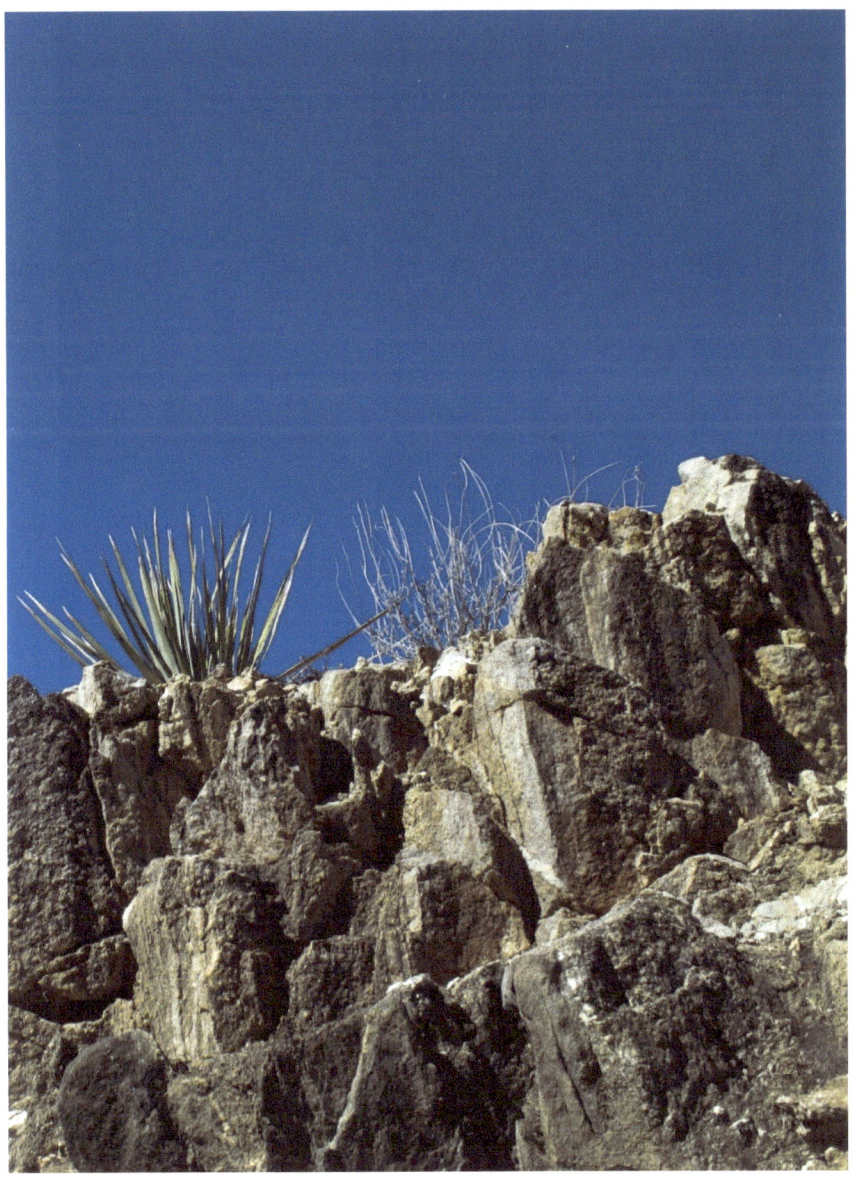

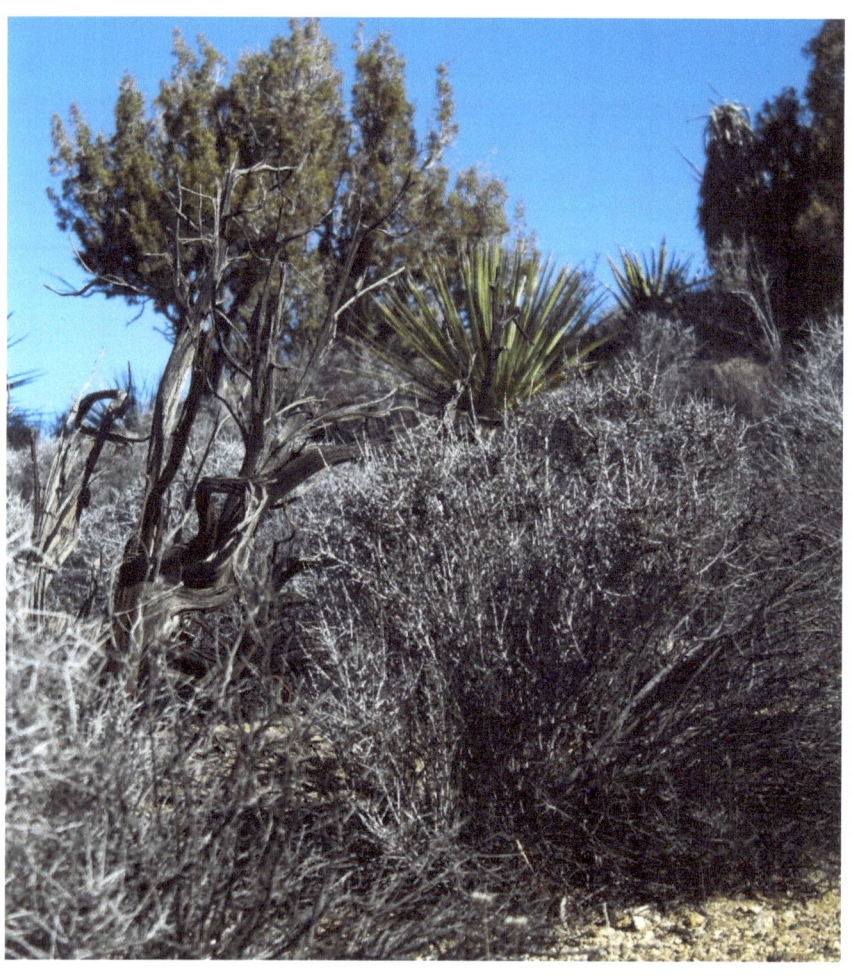

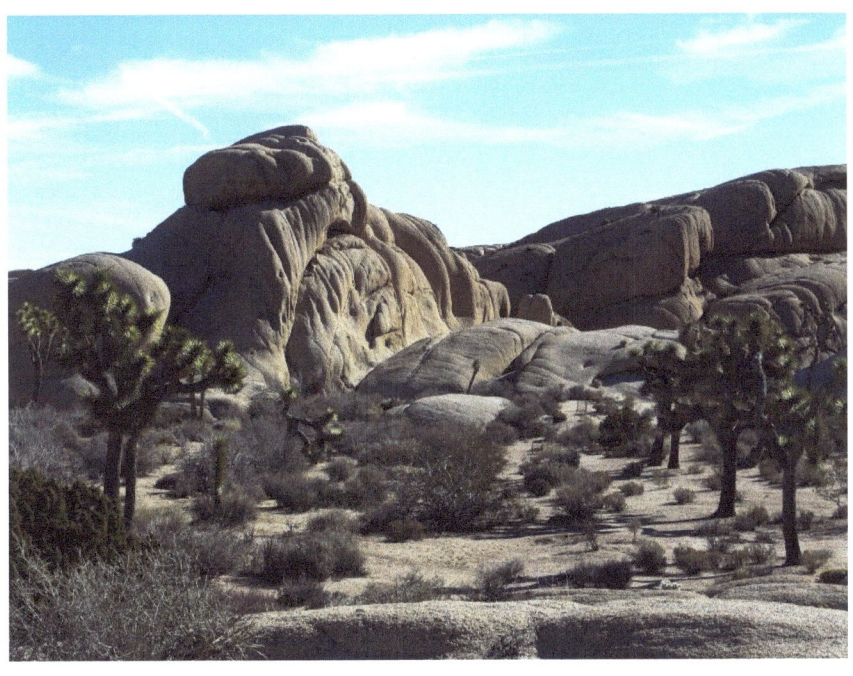

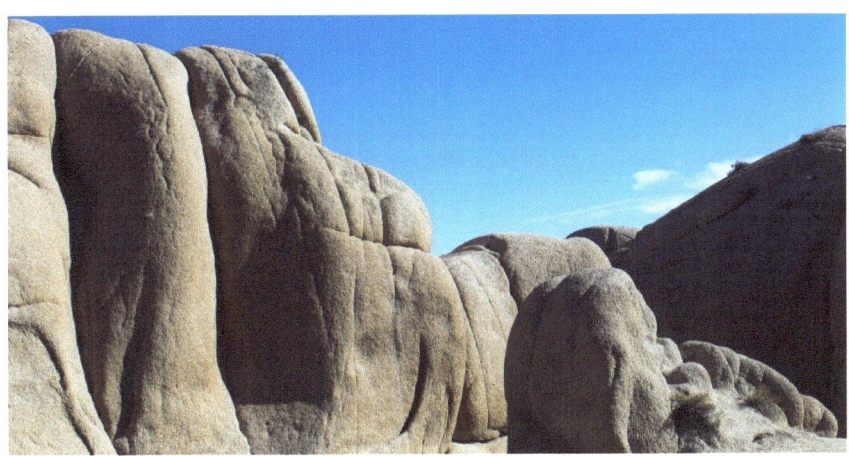

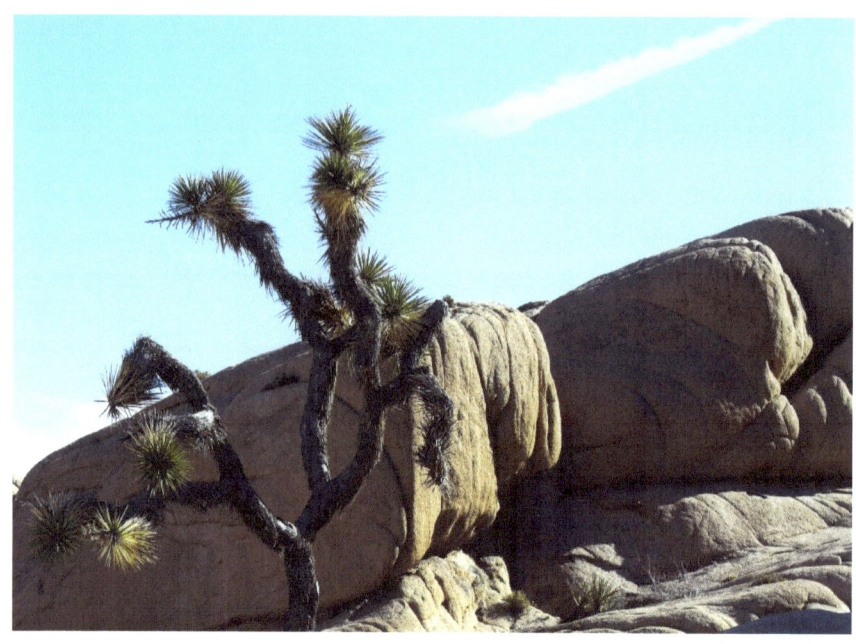

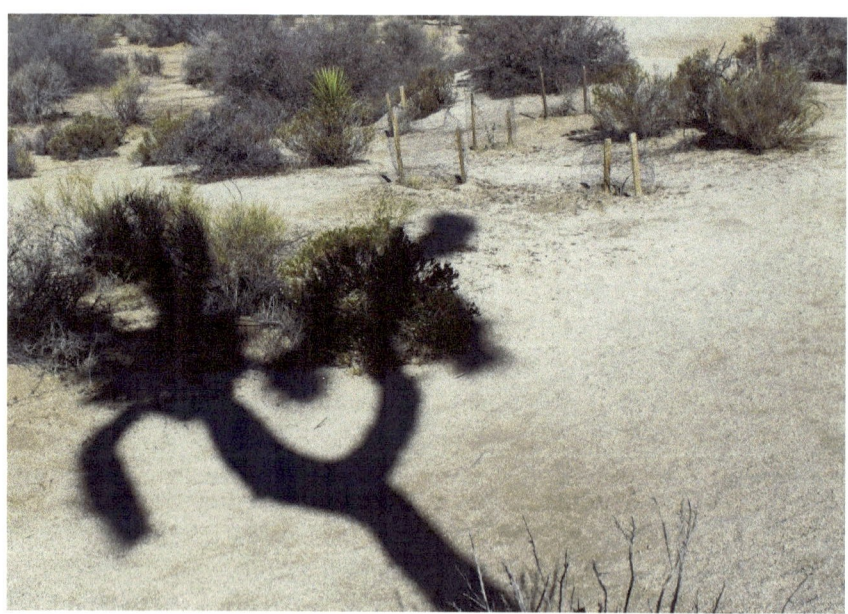

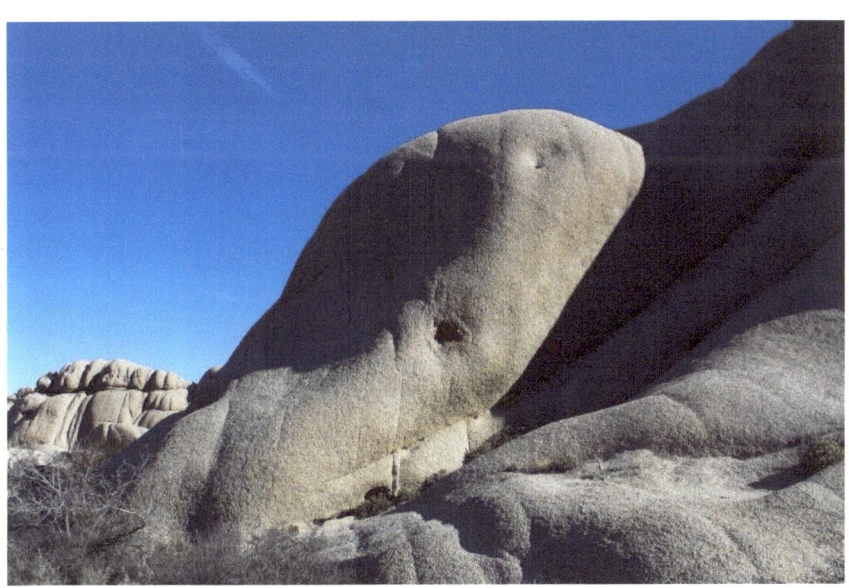

A rock that looks like a snake's head

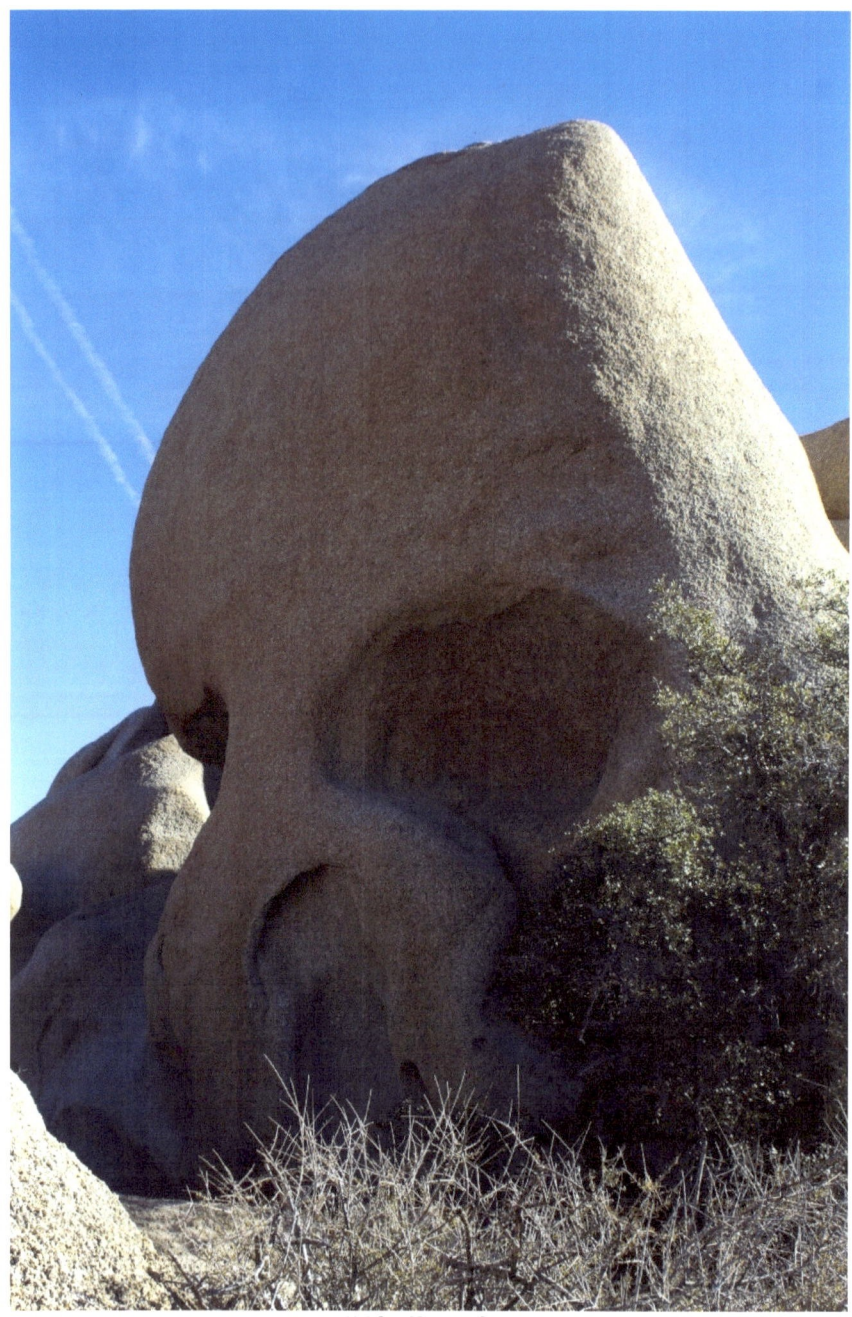

"Skull Rock"

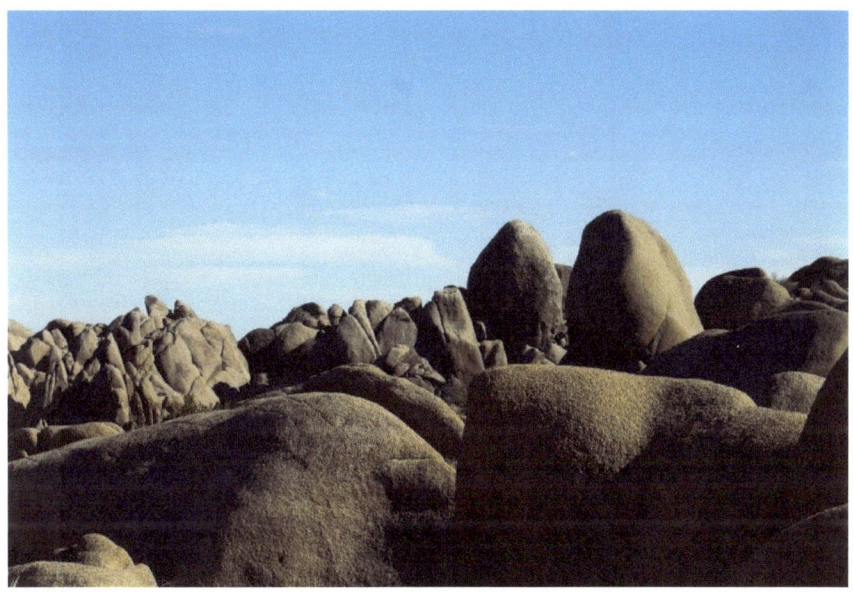

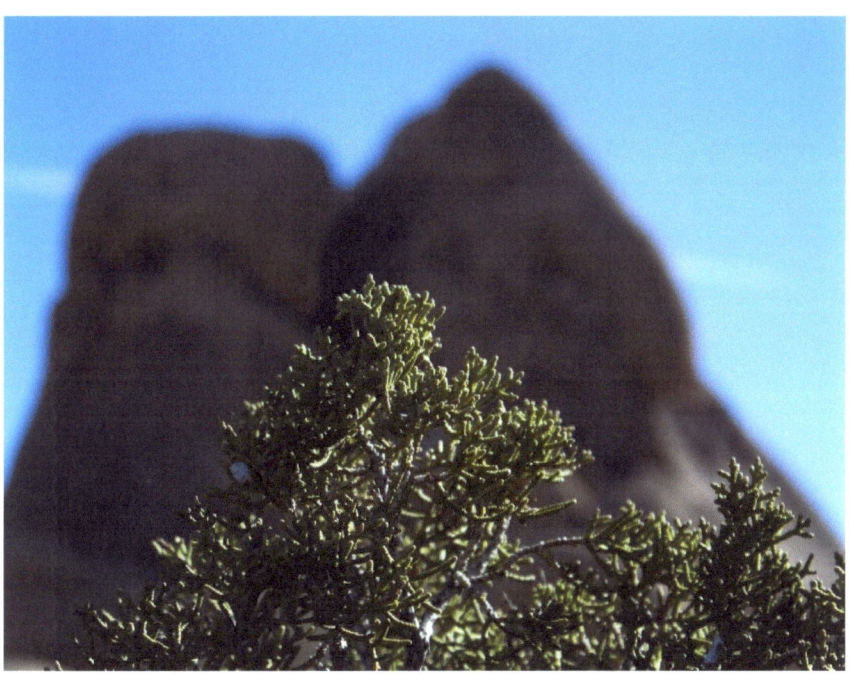

Tree mountain in front of the rock mountain

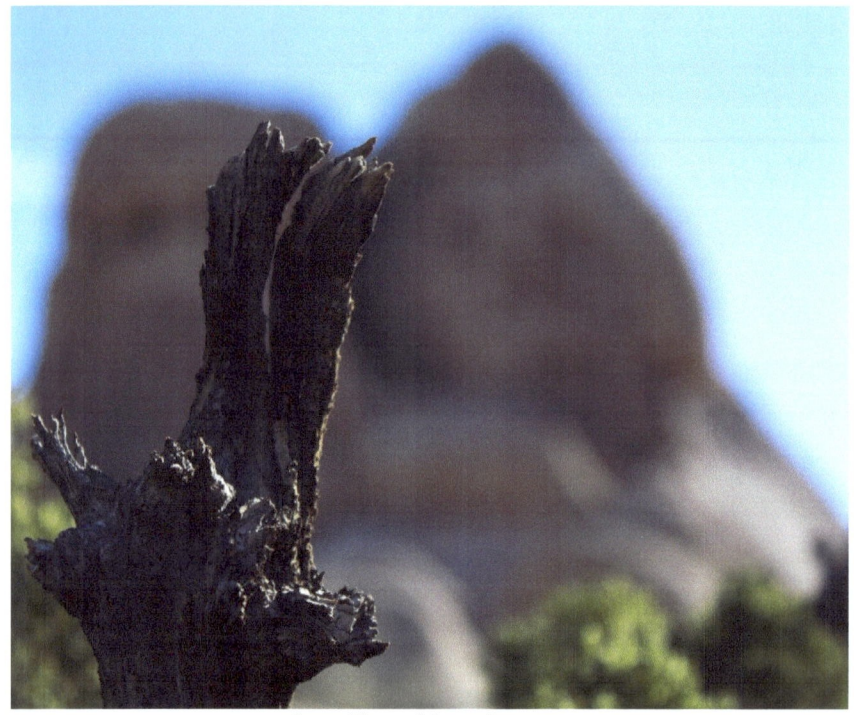

An old and lonely tree

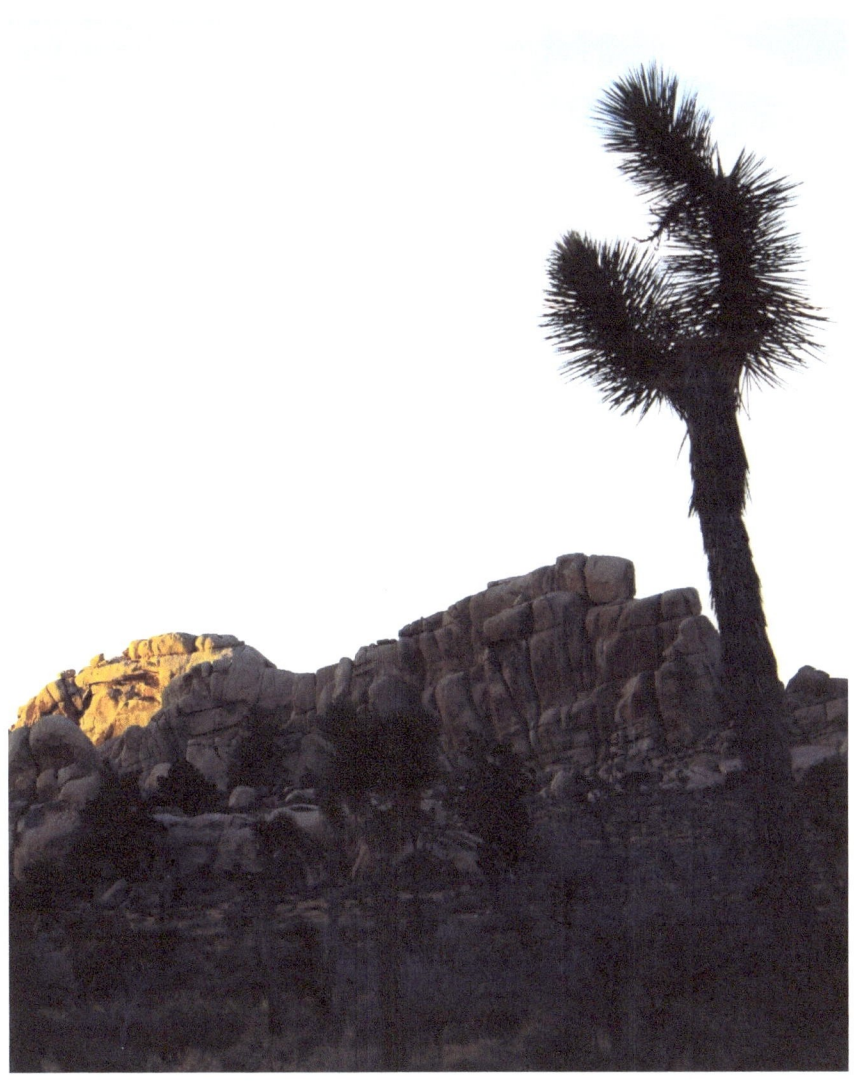

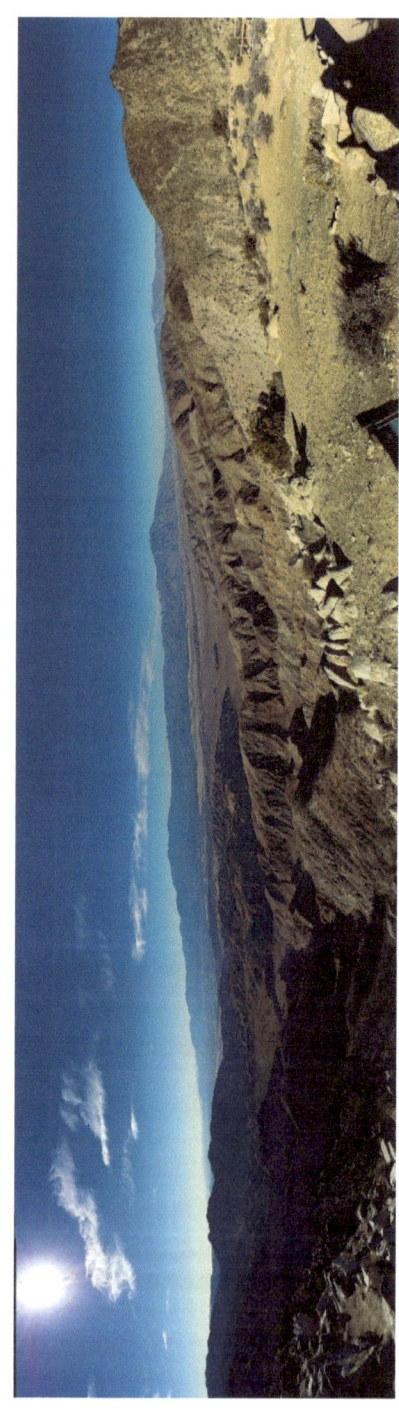

"Key's View" at the crest of the Little San Bernardino Mountains

Salton Sea

The Salton Sea is one of the world's largest inland seas and, at 227 feet (69.19 m) below sea level, one of the lowest spots on earth. The sea is approximately 35 miles (56.33 km) long, 15 miles (24.14 km) wide and 30 feet (9.14 m) deep. It began forming in 1905 when a construction crew working on the Colorado River created a breach in the river that caused water to flow into the Salton Trough. The flow of river water into the trough continued for 18 months until it was finally stopped by engineers dumping boulders into the breach.

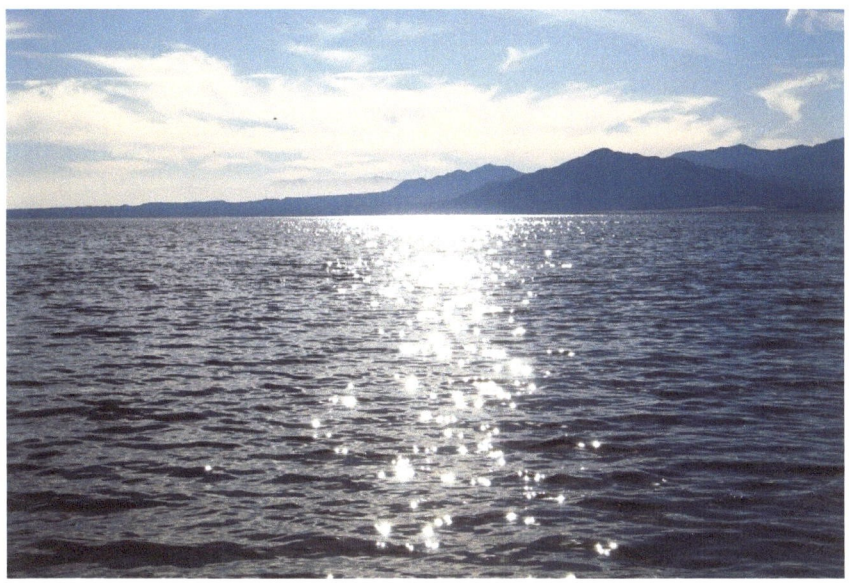

The Salton Sea has an extremely high content of salt. Its salt content is actually higher than that of the Pacific Ocean. Due to the high salt content, very few fish species can live in the Salton Sea. Since other freshwater fish species live in the rivers and canals that flow into the Salton Sea, when some of those fish end up in the sea, they die and wash up to the shore. As a result of this situation, the shores of the Salton Sea are cluttered with dead fish and fish skeletons. Unlike other beaches, which are covered with sand, the Salton Sea beaches are covered with dead, dried up barnacles and tiny, crushed fish bones.

Before going to Salton Sea, I thought that it was a pretty weird place because it is a big lake with dead fish on the shore. After doing some research, it seemed even more interesting, so I wanted to go even more. Walking on the beach was really strange. The beach was not hard like sand. It was soft, and felt like my feet might sink in, but they didn't. After I went, I thought it was very funny after actually seeing all the dead fish and because the smell was terrible. I have never smelled anything that bad.

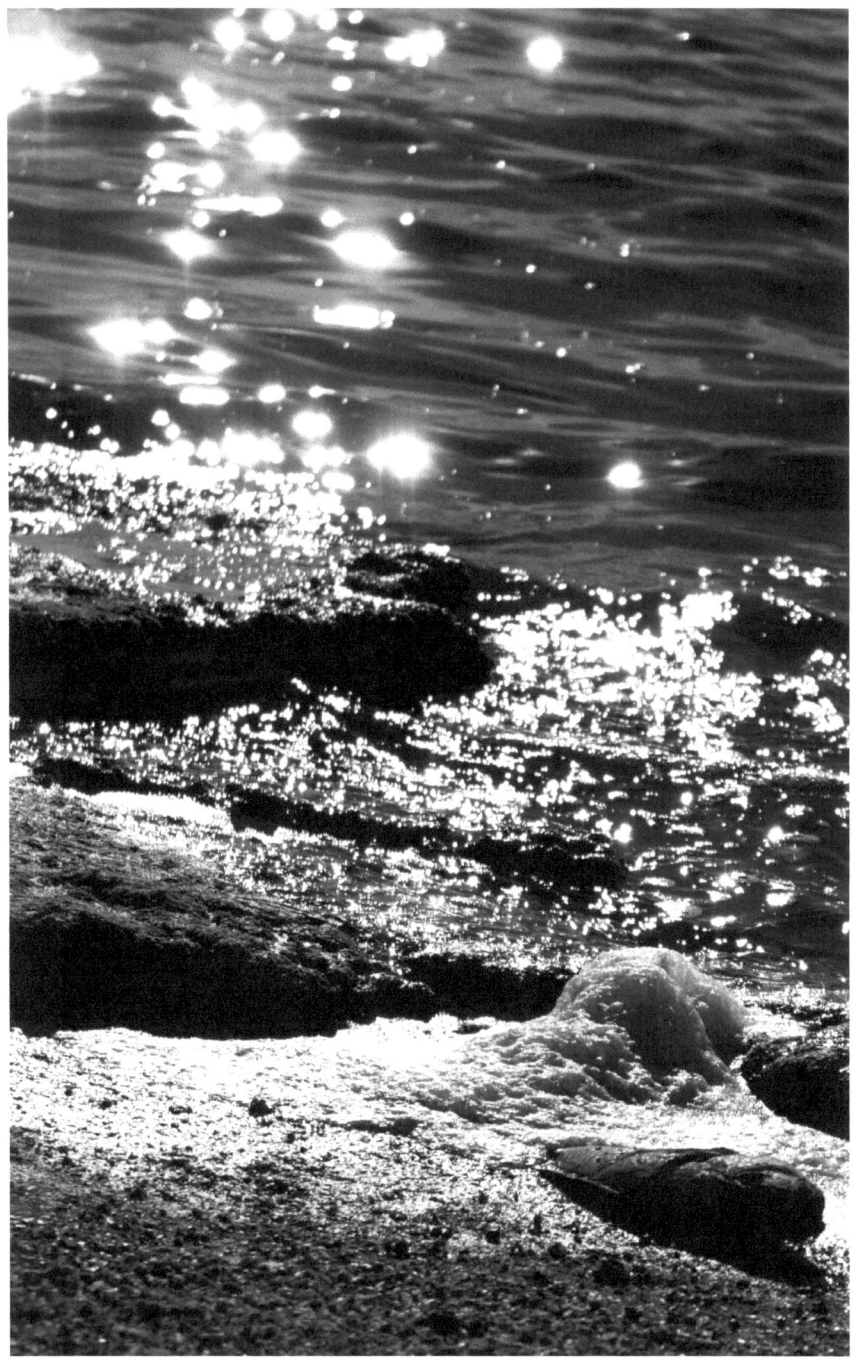

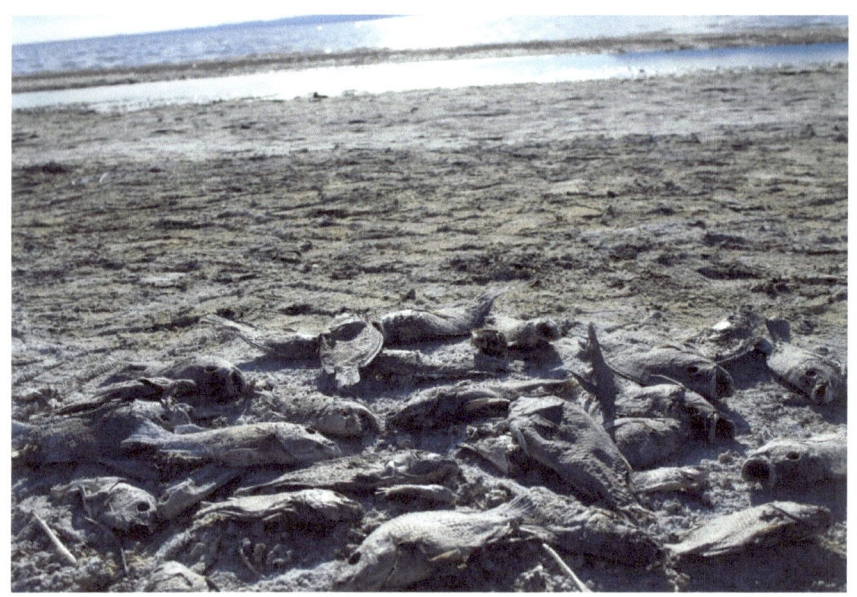

A school of dead fish (during recess)

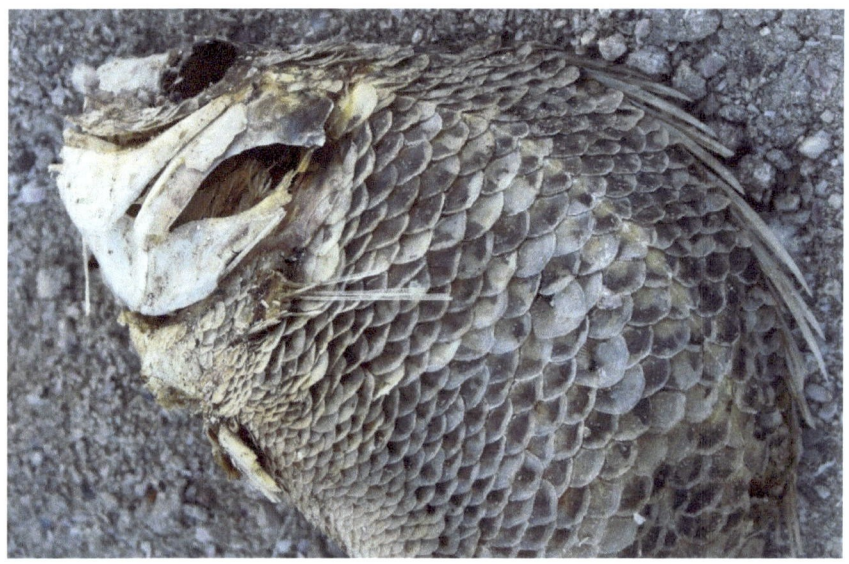

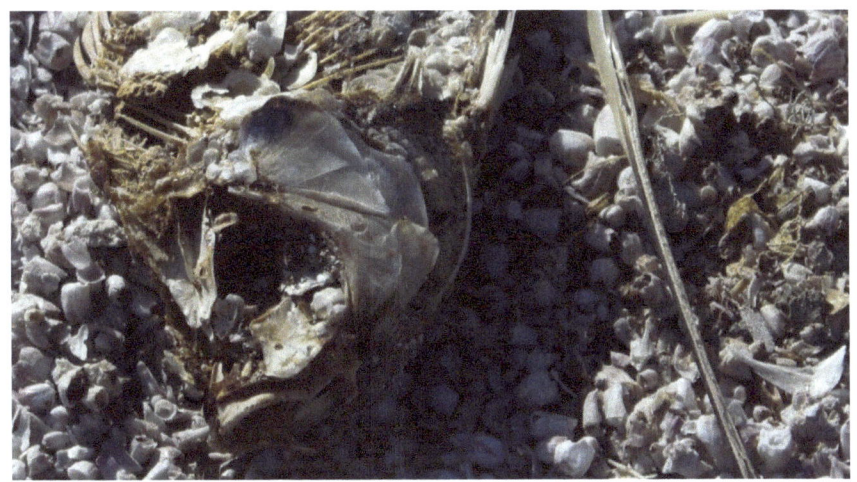

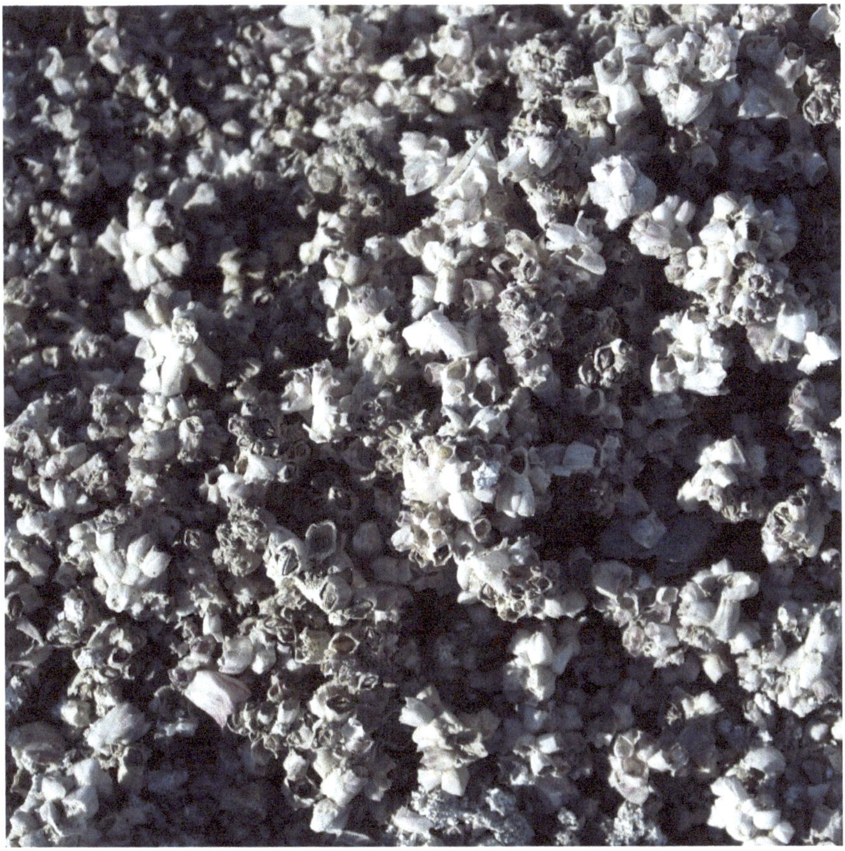

The Salton Sea Beach (dried up barnacles)

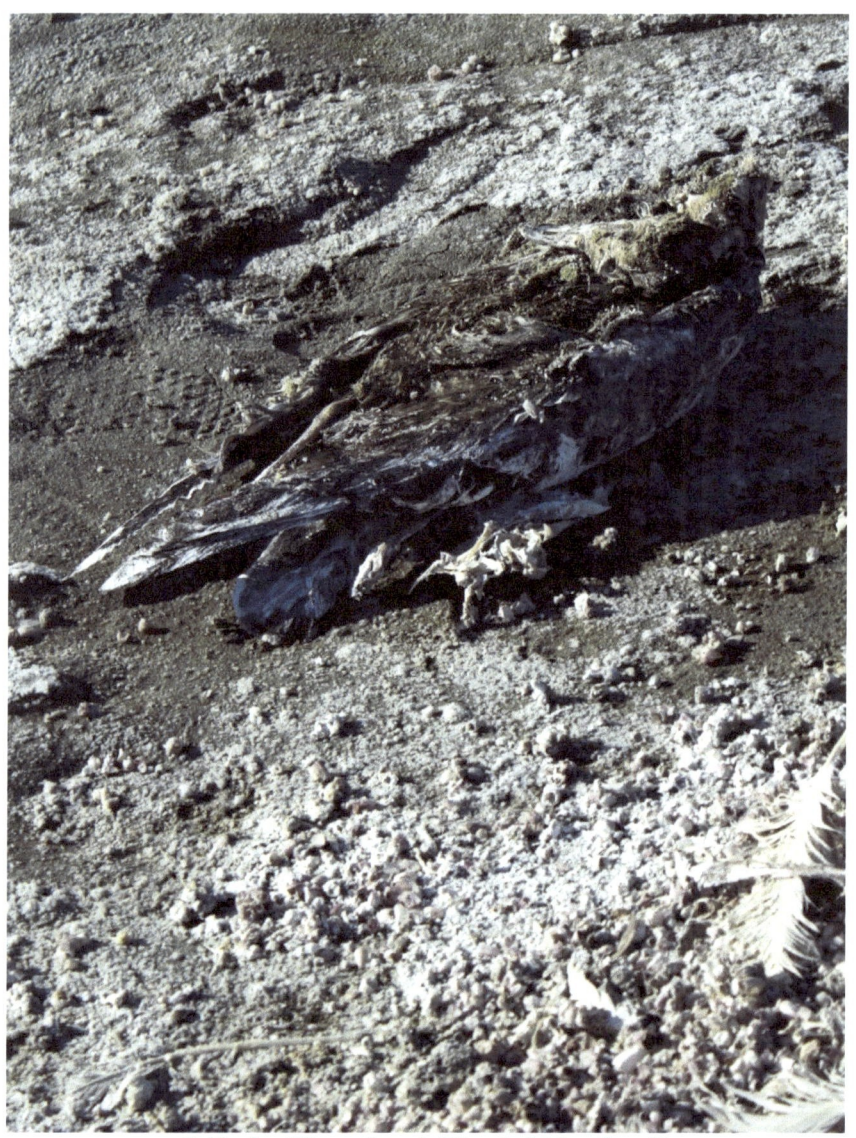

A bird with no head (it might be dead)

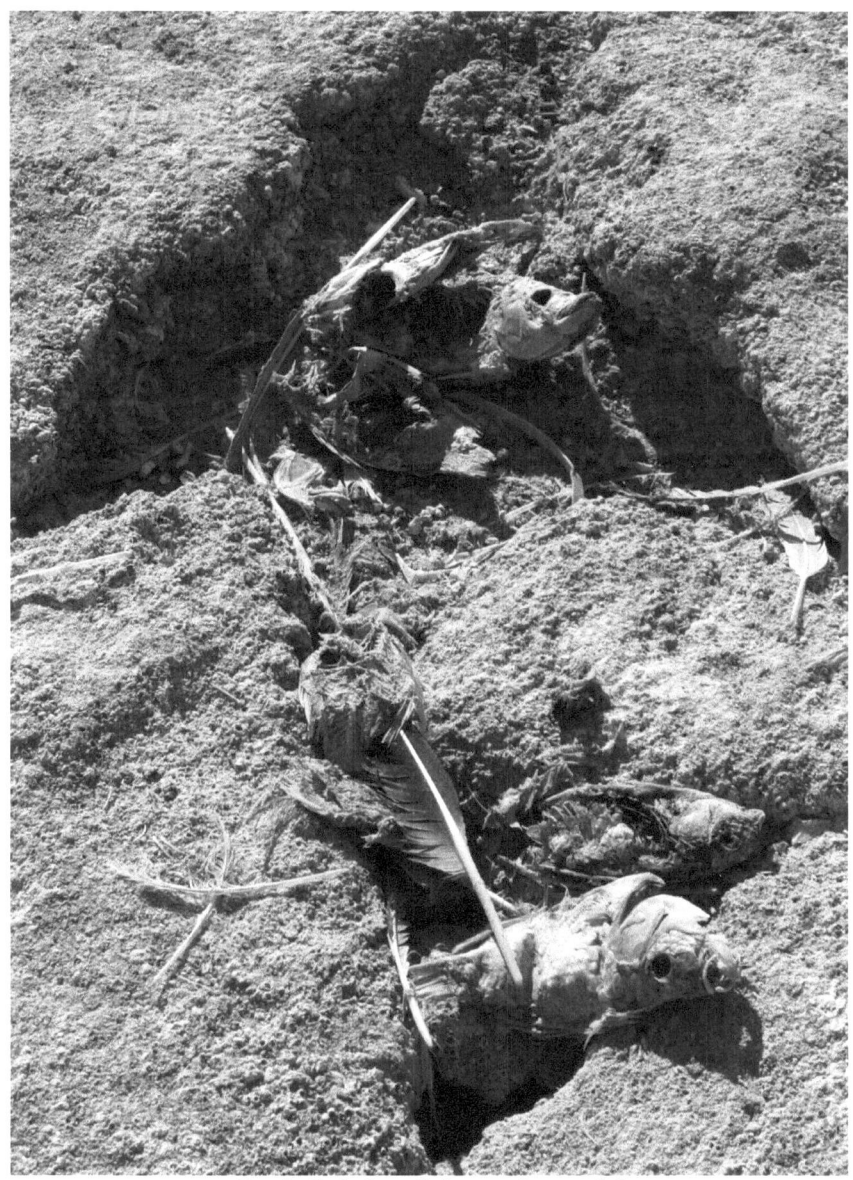

Rock fish (or fish on the rock)

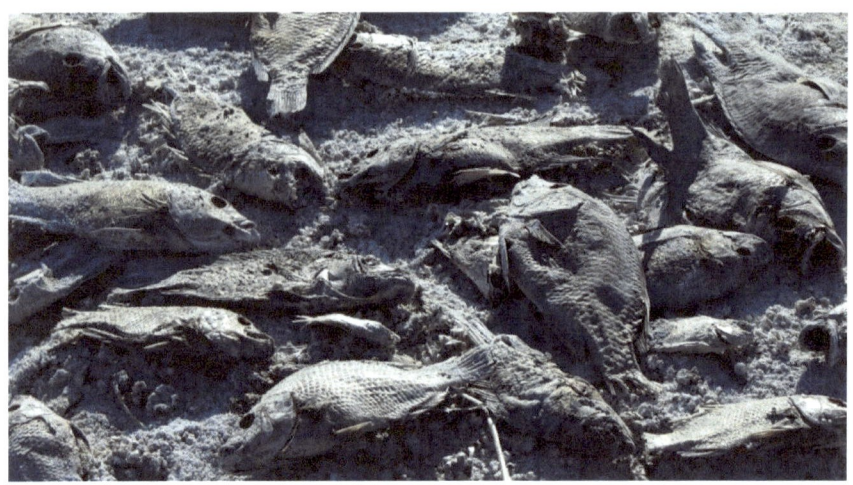

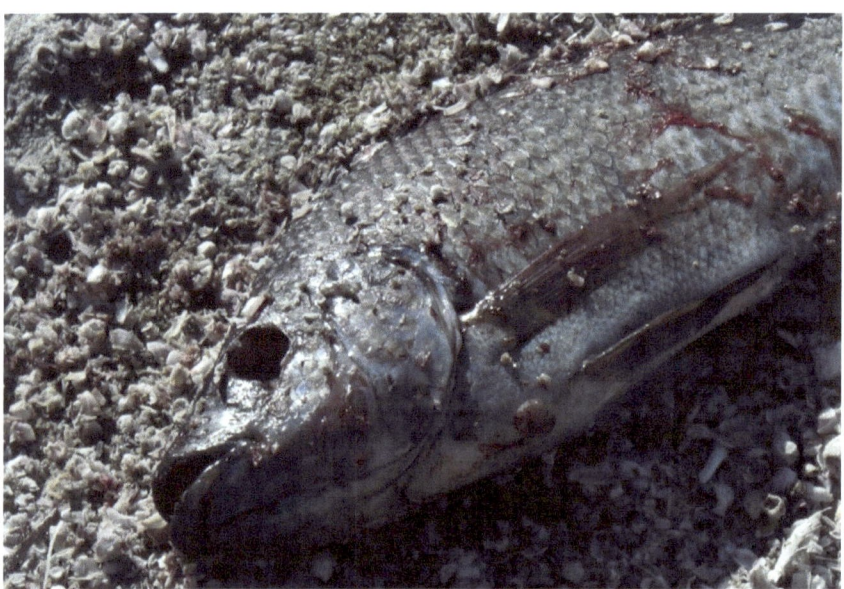

Birds eat the fish eyes (maybe I should try it)

Salvation Mountain

Salvation Mountain is located on a hill in the Colorado Desert, approximately 81 miles (130 km) southeast of Palms Springs, California. The mountain is artwork made from adobe, straw and thousands of gallons of lead-free paint. It is comprised of numerous murals and areas painted with Christian sayings and Bible verses. Salvation Mountain was created by Leonard Knight, who was a local resident of the area until his death in 2014 at the age of 82.

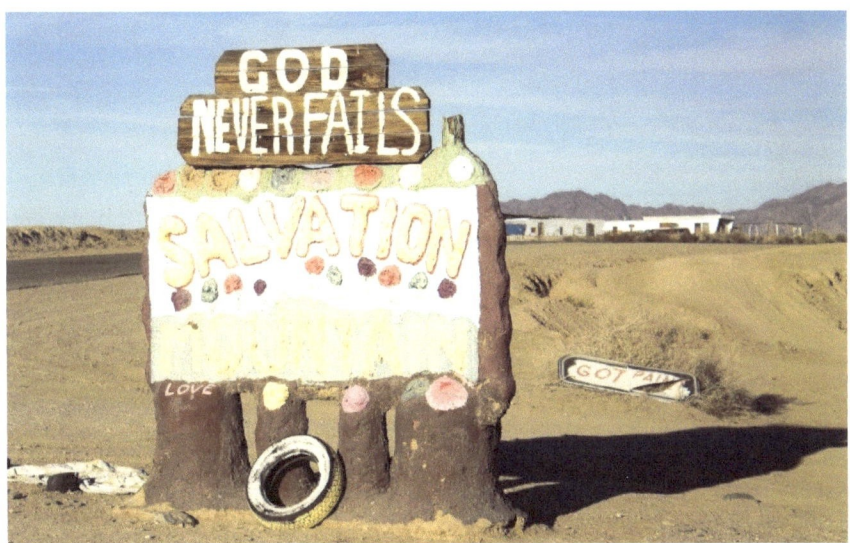

Entrance to Salvation Mountain

I thought Salvation Mountain was very cool. I've seen many pictures of the colorful mountain on the Internet, and wanted to go there some day. After seeing Salvation Mountain in person, I was very happy that I went. Many people I know have not been there so I was glad that I visited the mountain. It was very cool and very colorful. I was very fascinated by the fact that one guy thought of a way to show his love for god by using paint and a hill.

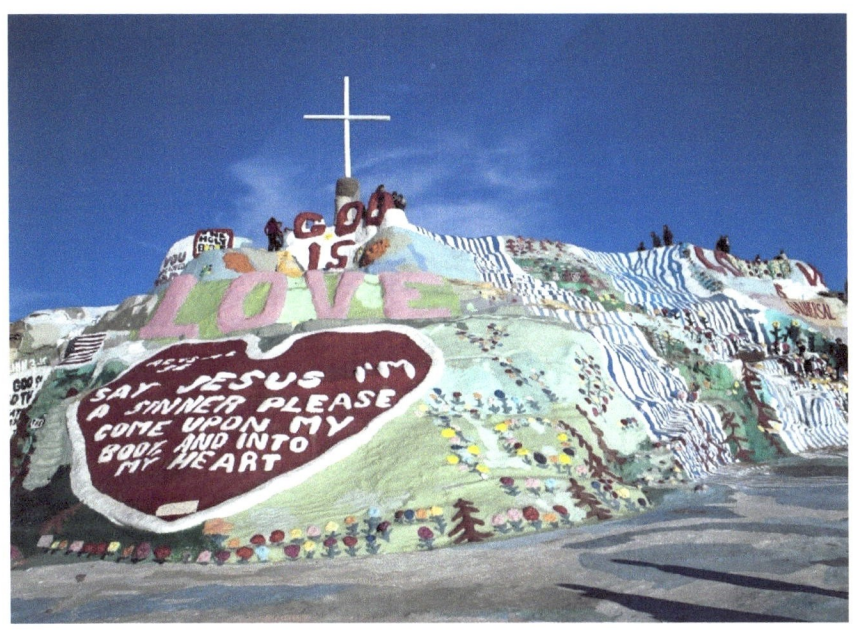

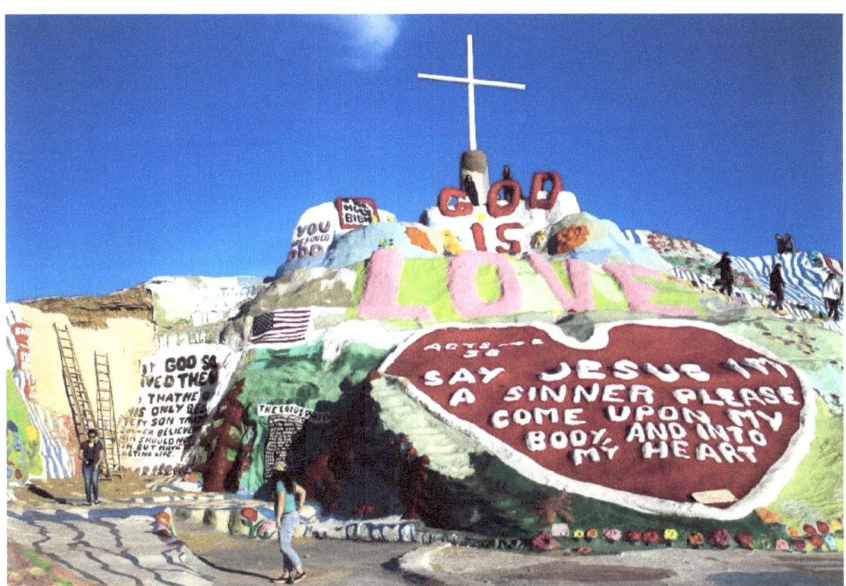

Salvation Mountain

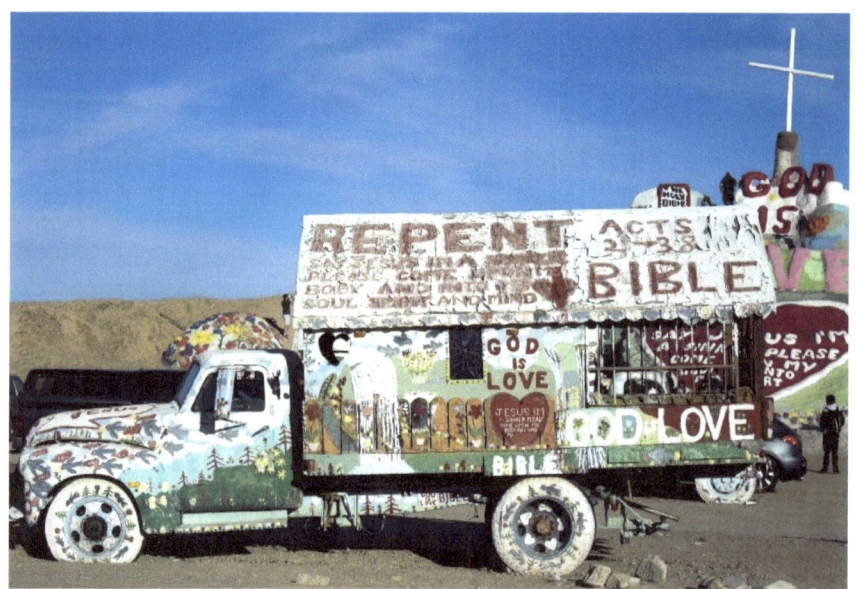

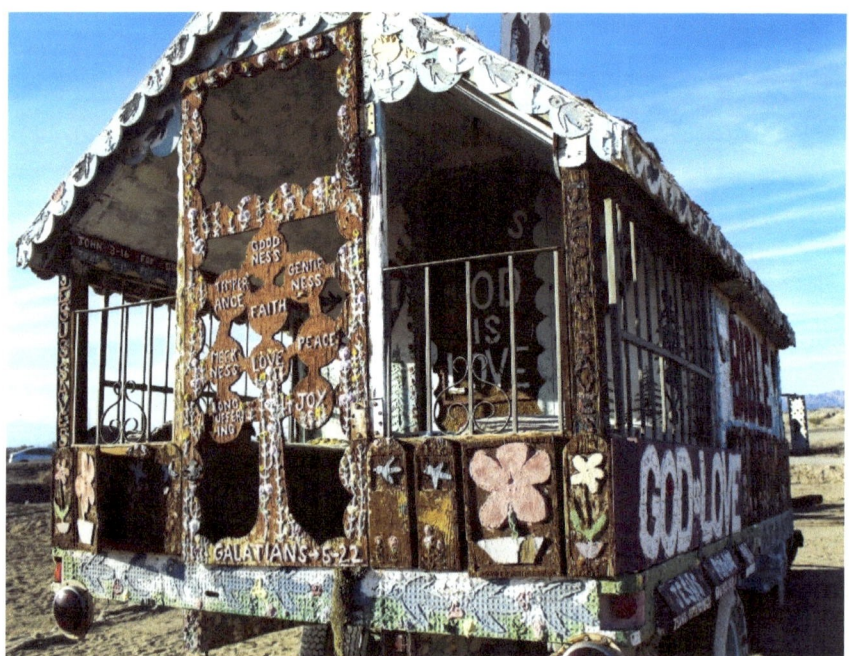

Salvation Mountain truck

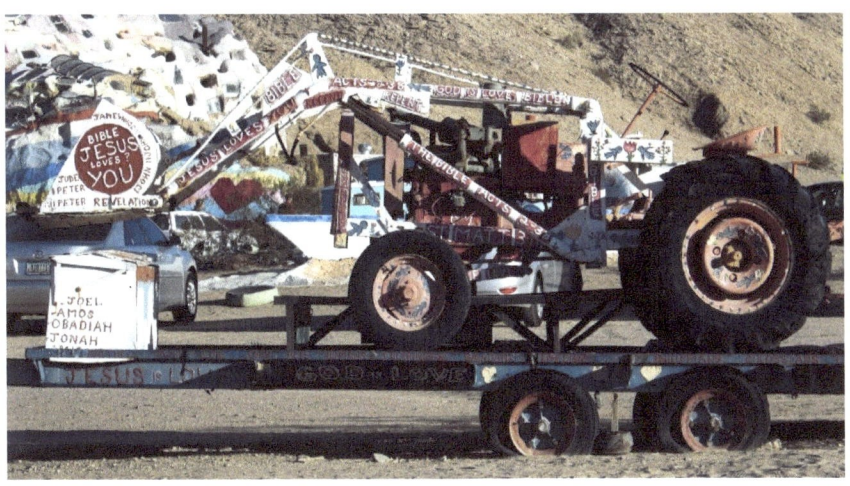

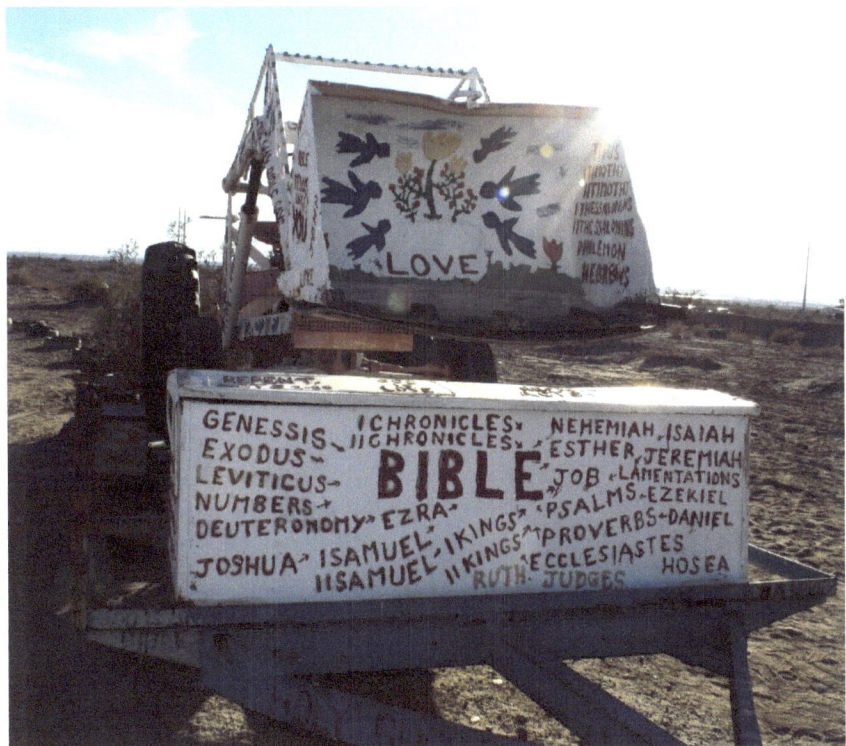

Salvation Mountain tractor

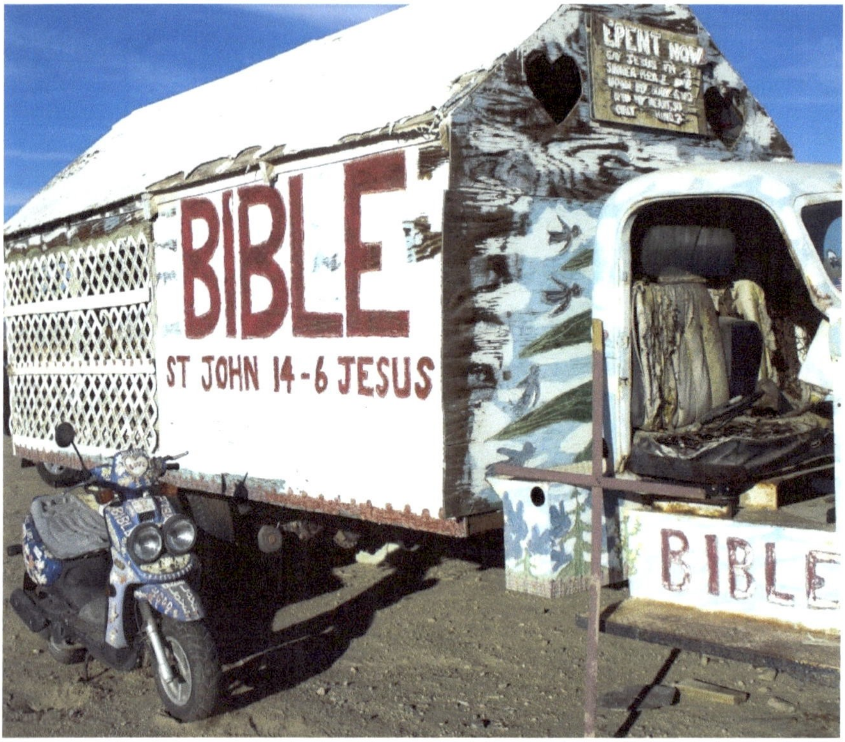

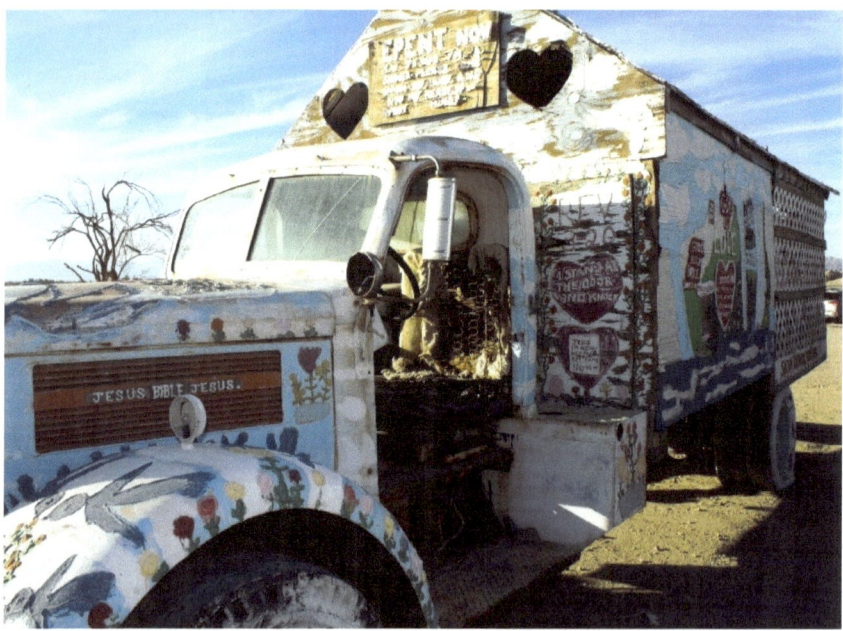

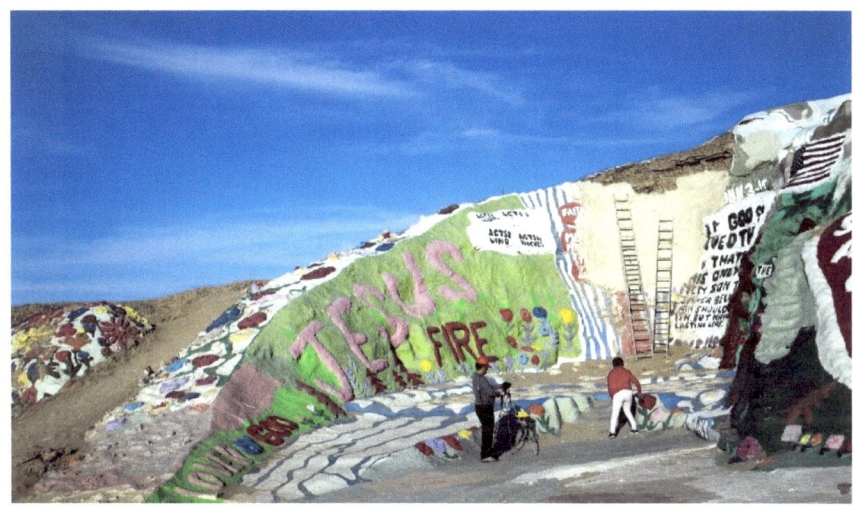

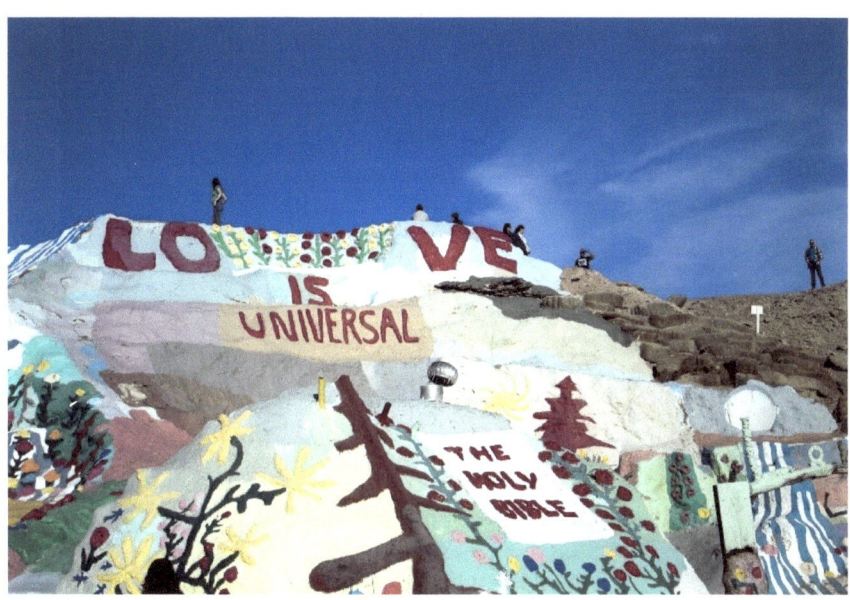

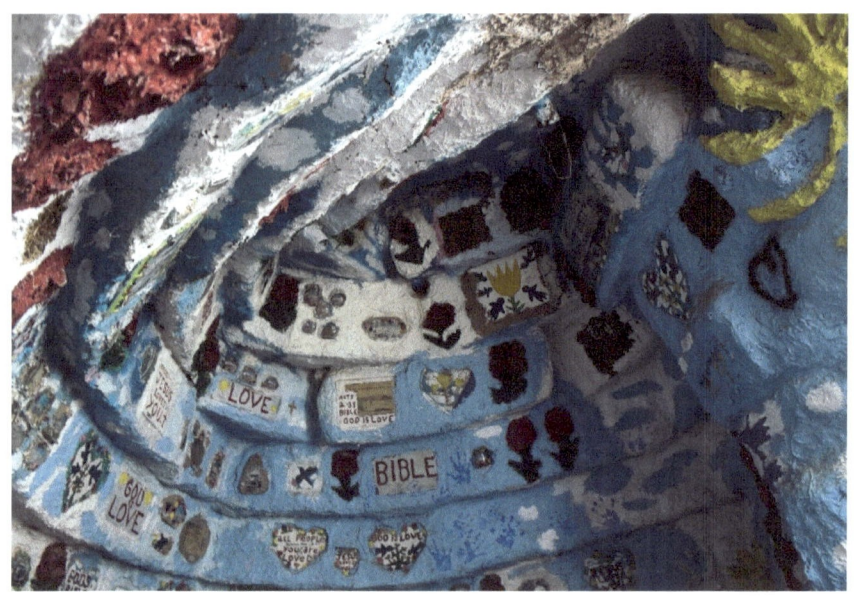

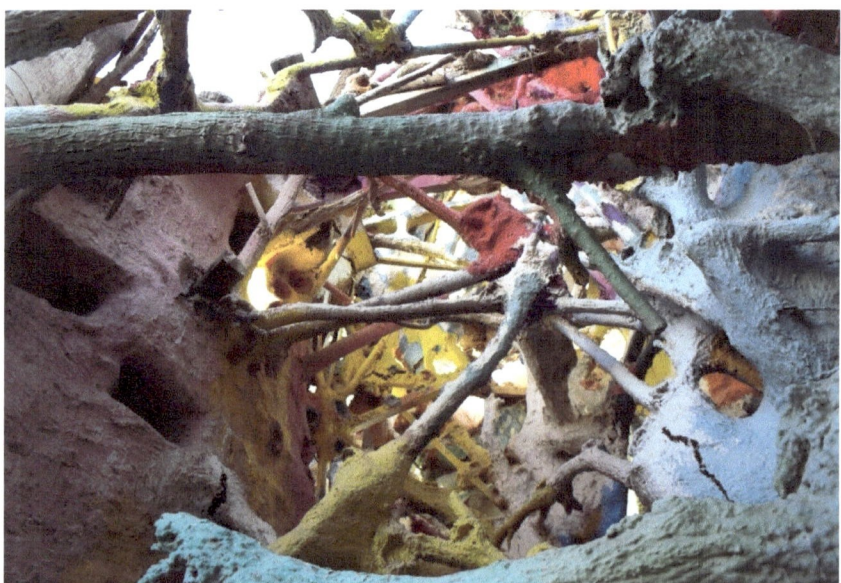

Inside the west side of the mountain

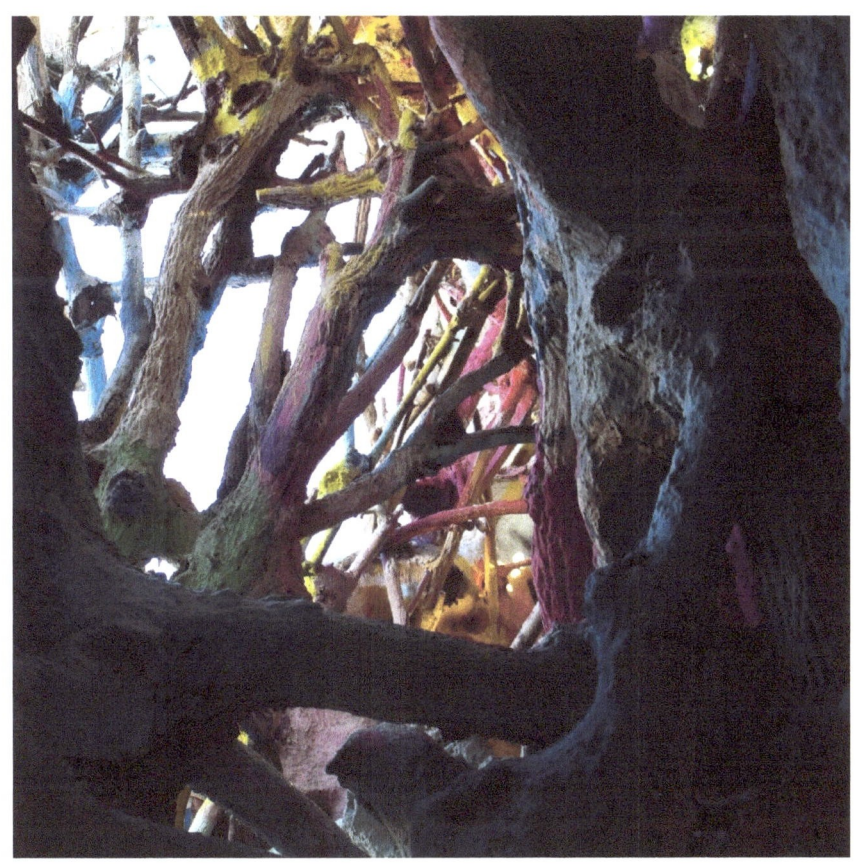

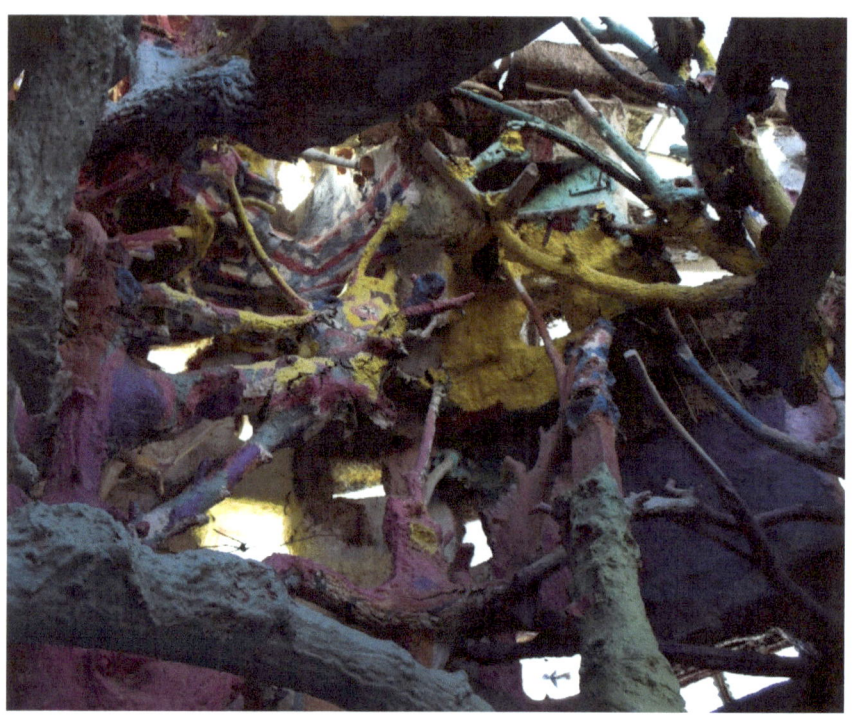

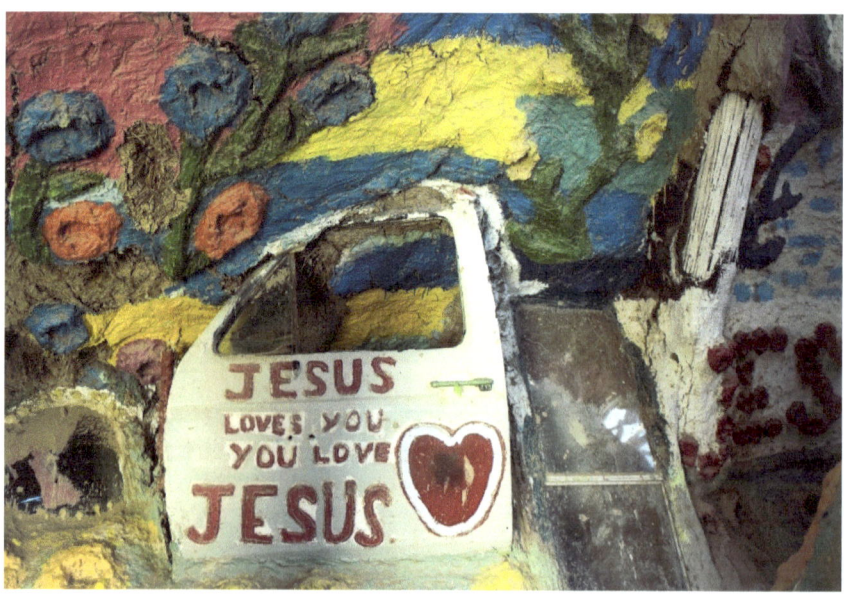

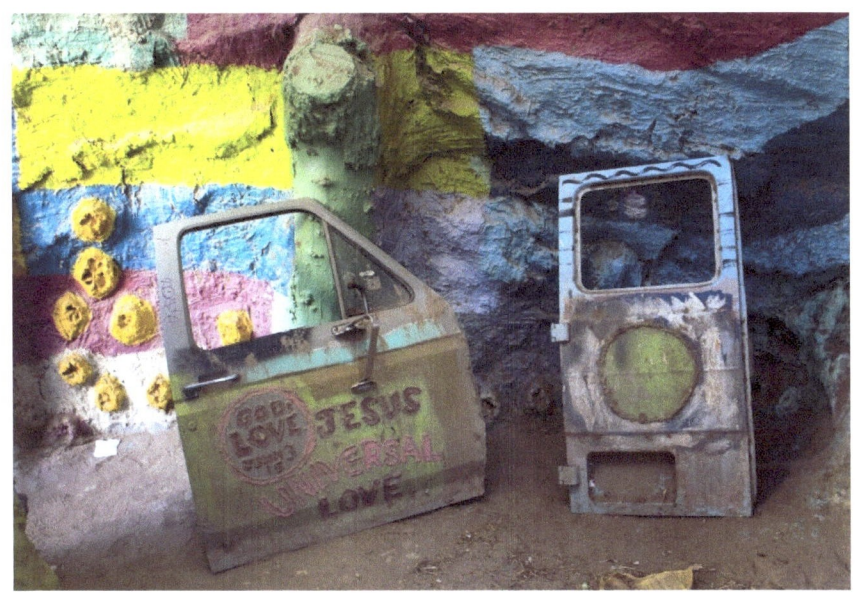

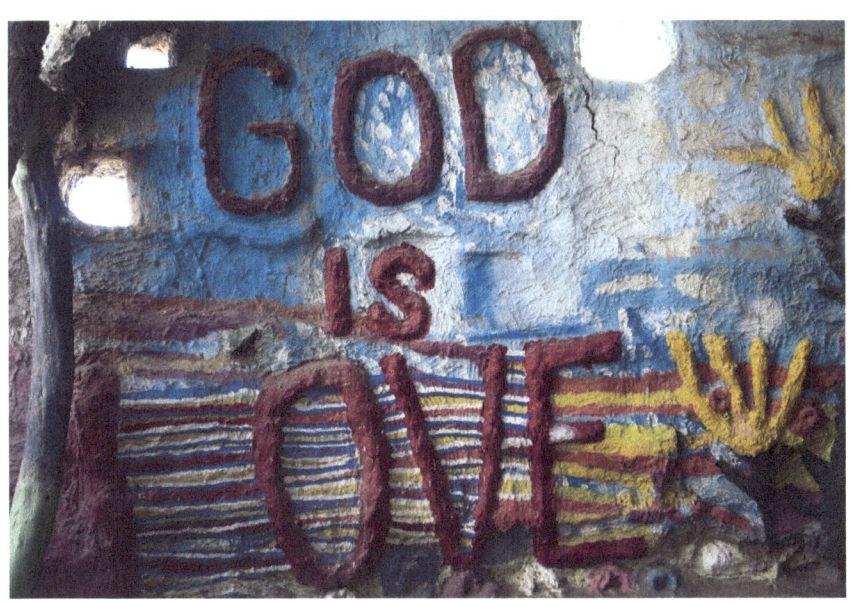

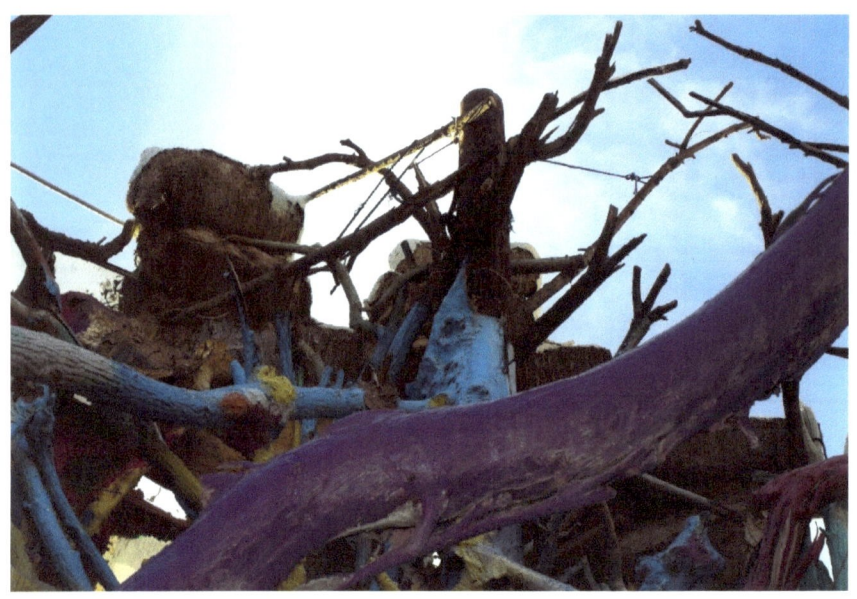

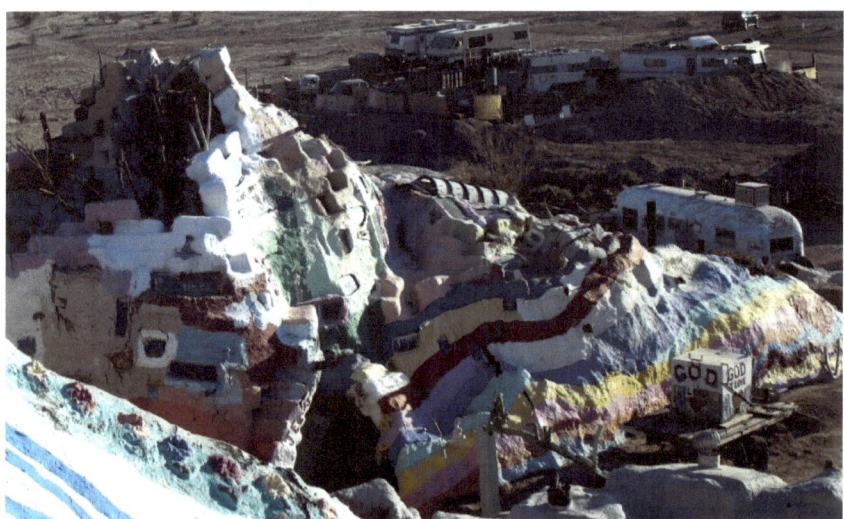

A view from the top of the mountain

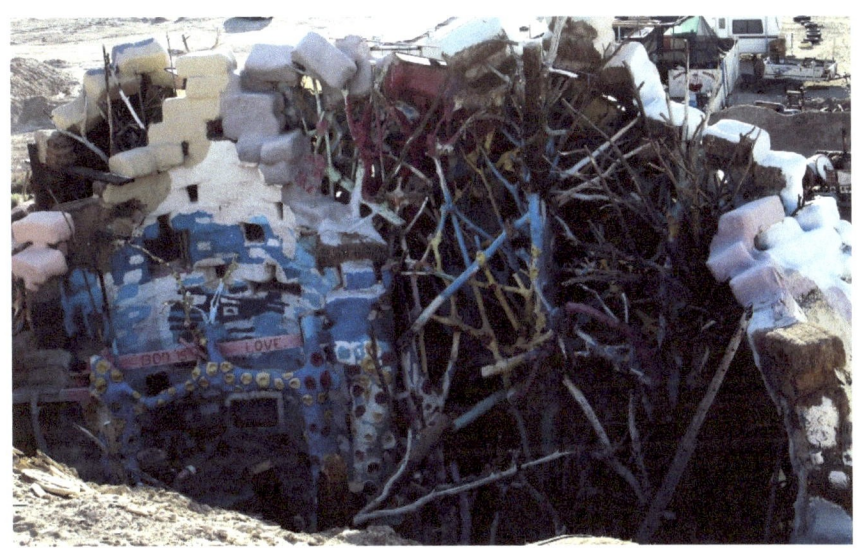

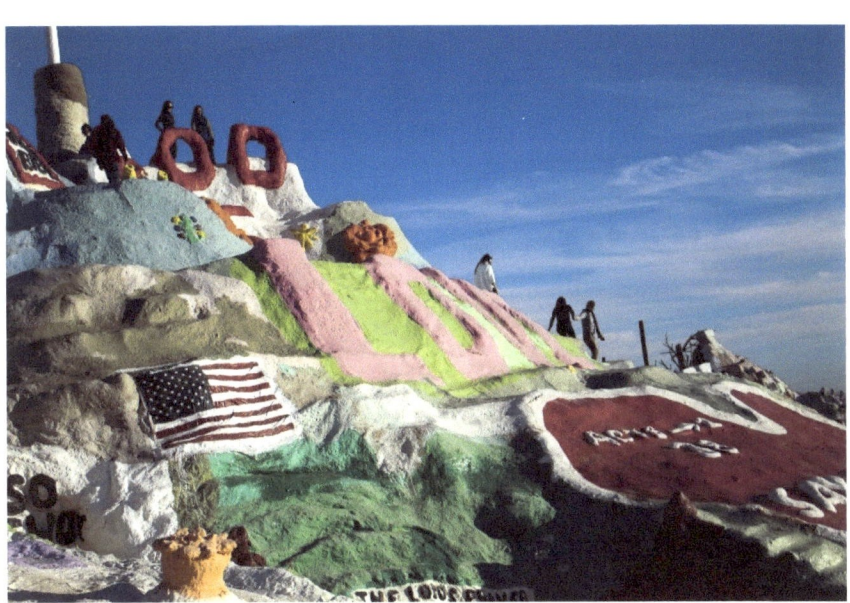

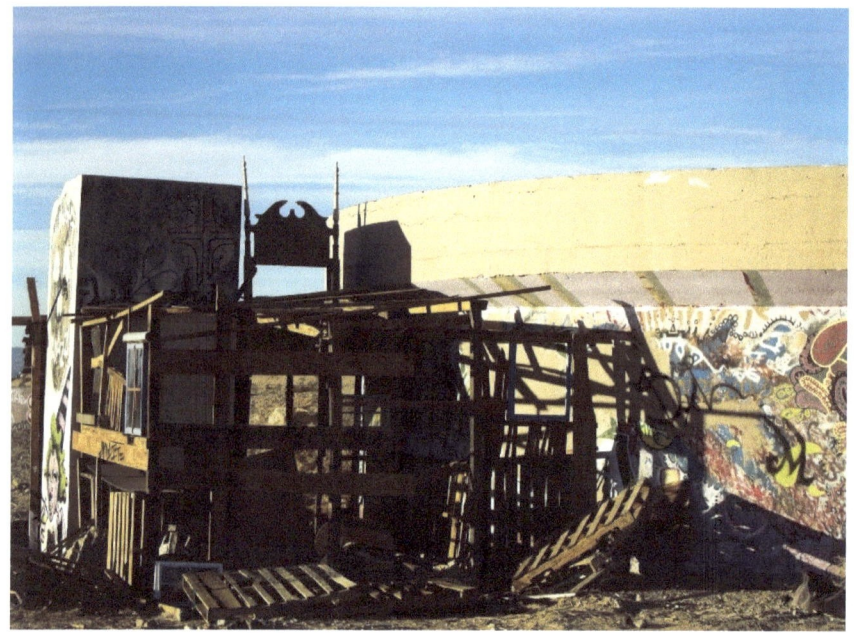

Salvation Mountain adjacent

Slab City, California

Slab City is a campsite located about 1.5 miles (2.4 km) east of Salvation Mountain. The site was originally a U.S. Marine Corps training base built in 1942. When the military base was closed in 1956, all of the buildings were removed. However, the slabs that the buildings sat on were not removed. That is the reason why the area is called "Slab City".

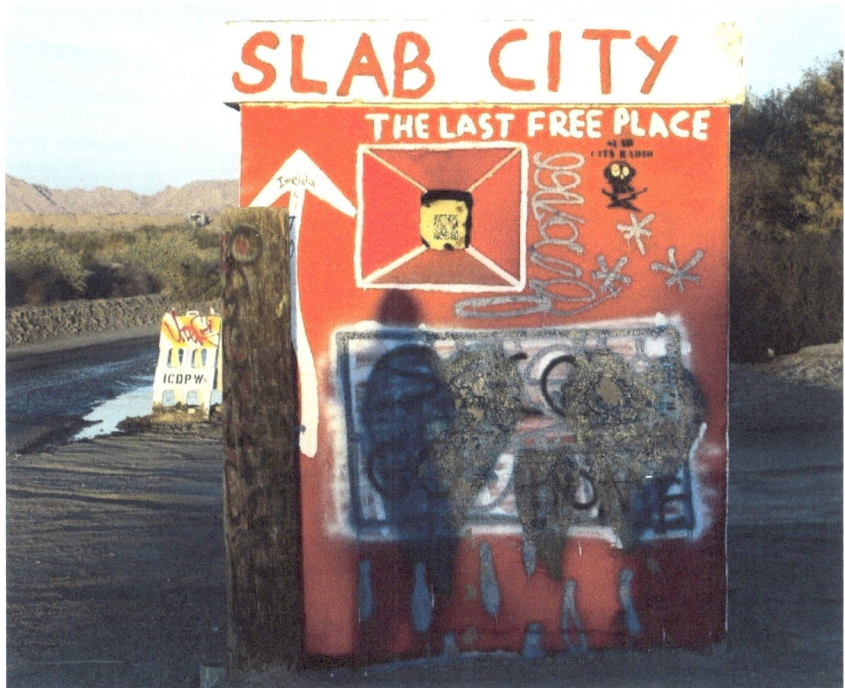

Slab City is used by recreational vehicle owners and squatters from across America. Since the summer temperatures can reach as high as 120 °F (48 °C), most campers stay at the site only during the winter months, and travel north in the summer. However, there are some permanent residents who live there year round. In addition to campers, Slab City attracts people who want to live "off-the-grid" and want to be left alone. It has no electricity, no running water, no sewers nor toilets and no trash pickup service.

East Jesus

East Jesus is an area in Slab City. it is not called East Jesus because of anything related to religion. The term "East Jesus" is an old slang that refers to places in the "middle of nowhere". It is primarily an art community. Many sculptures are created using materials that have been reused, recycled or repurposed.

My first impression of Slab City was that it was a city with absolutely nothing. I thought that there were a lot of weird people in trailers living there. Slab City is considered the last free place in the United States. I did not want to go there because I thought it was dangerous and scary. After visiting the city, I was glad I went. The place called East Jesus is where people made art out of junk. I thought it was very cool.

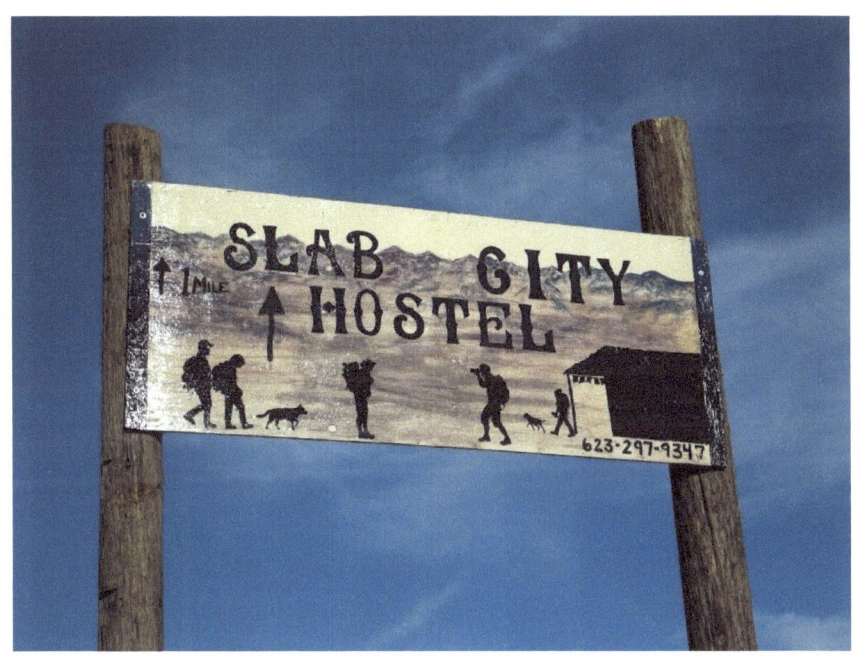

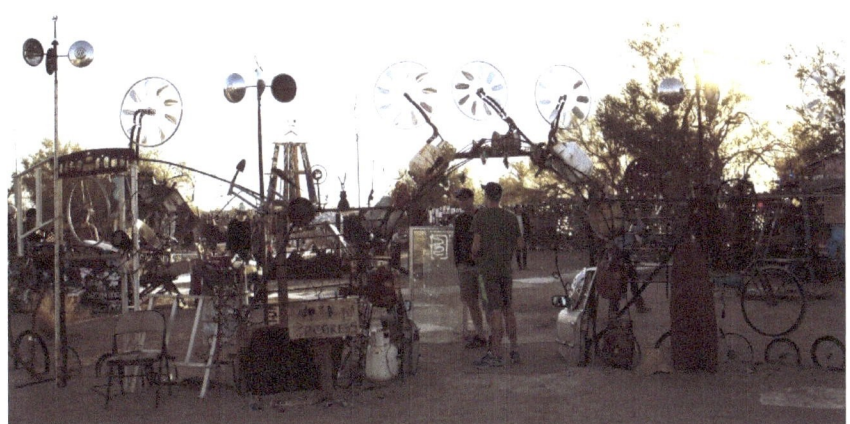

East Jesus sculpture garden entry

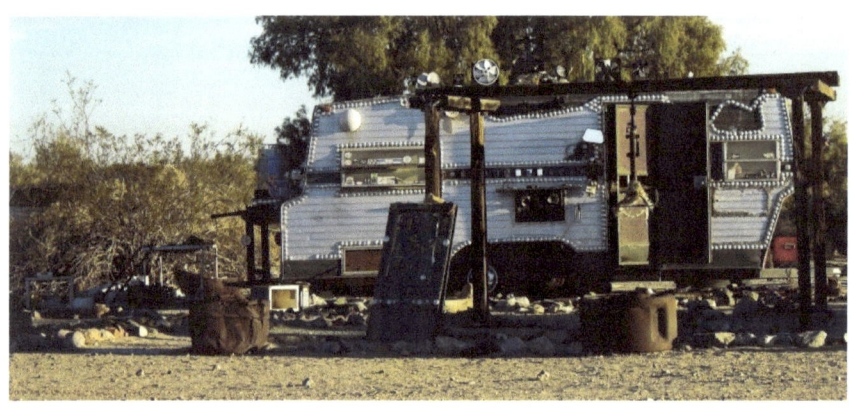

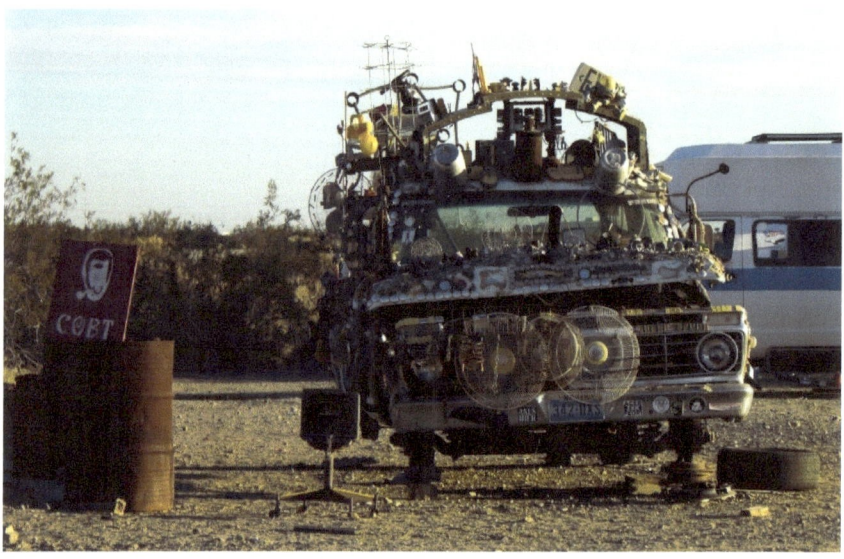

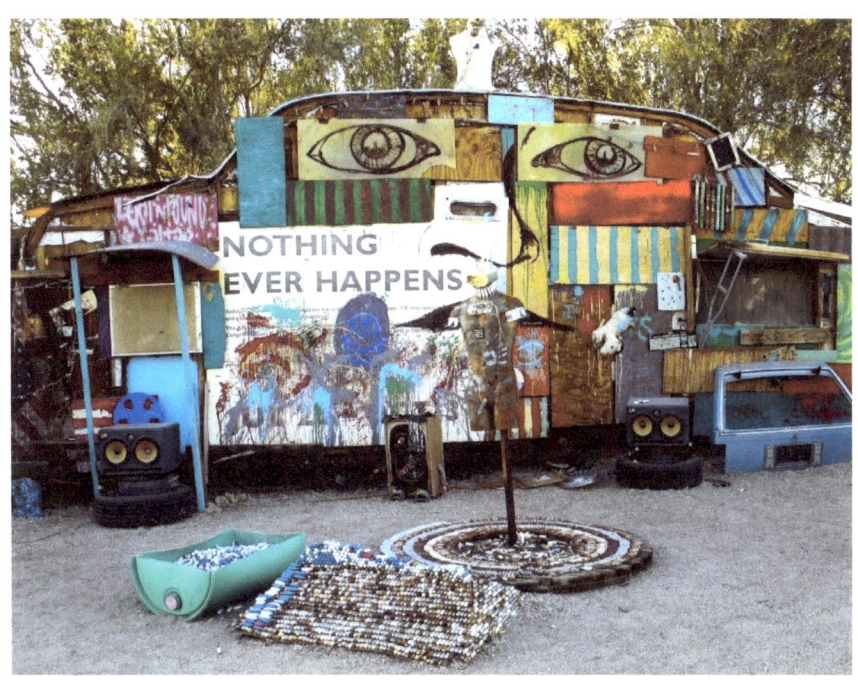

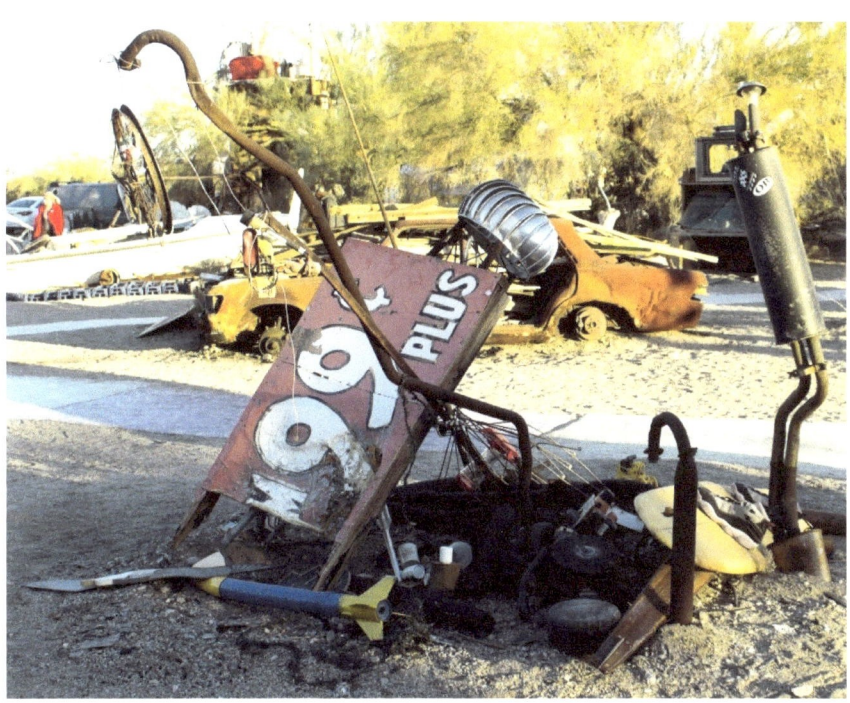

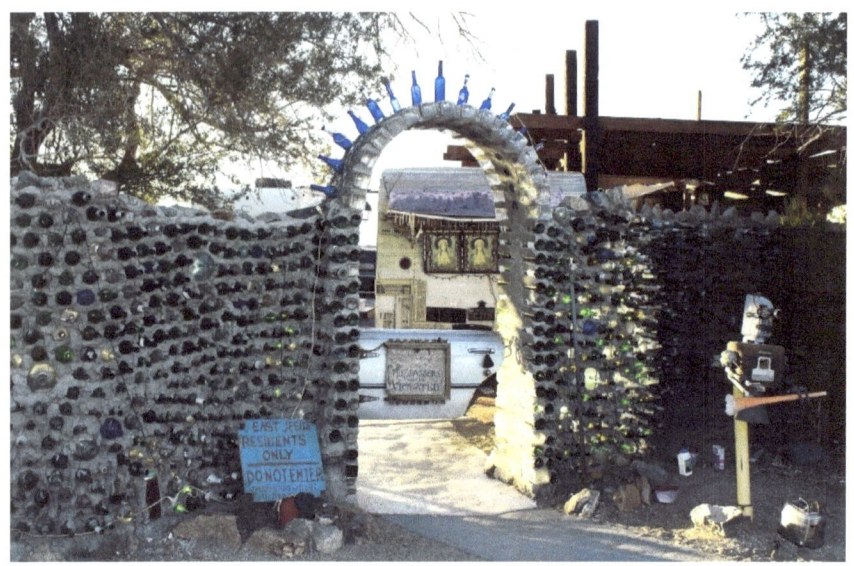

"Bottle Wall"

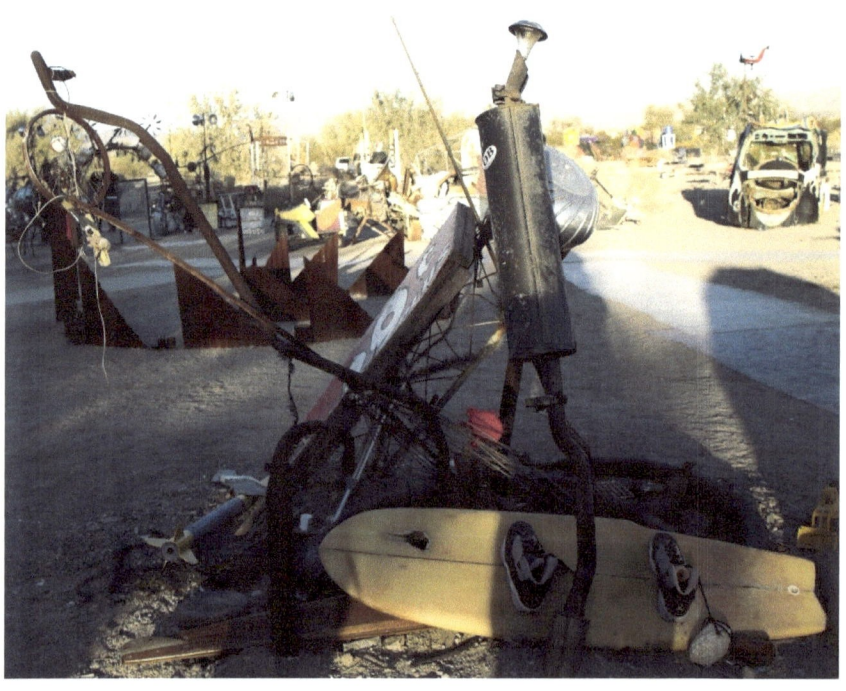

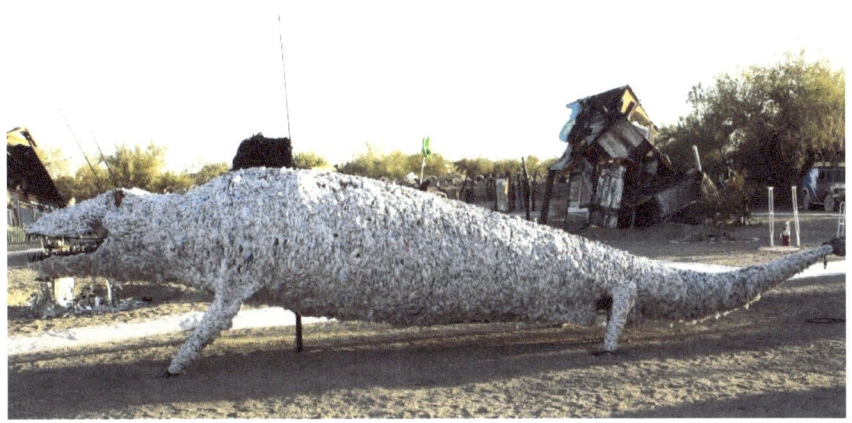

Dinosaur made from plastic trash bags

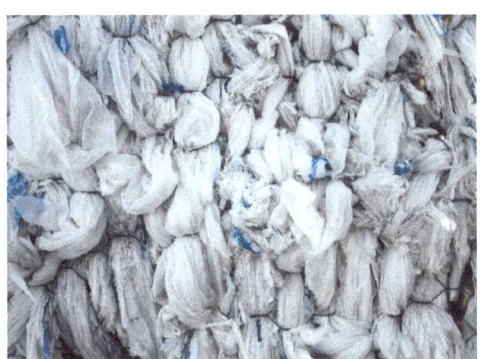

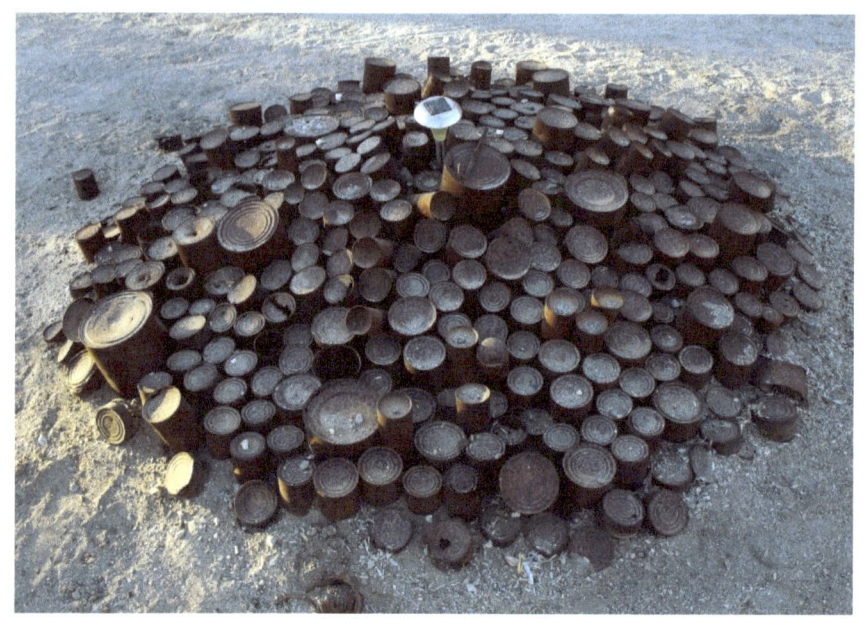

"The Can Organ"

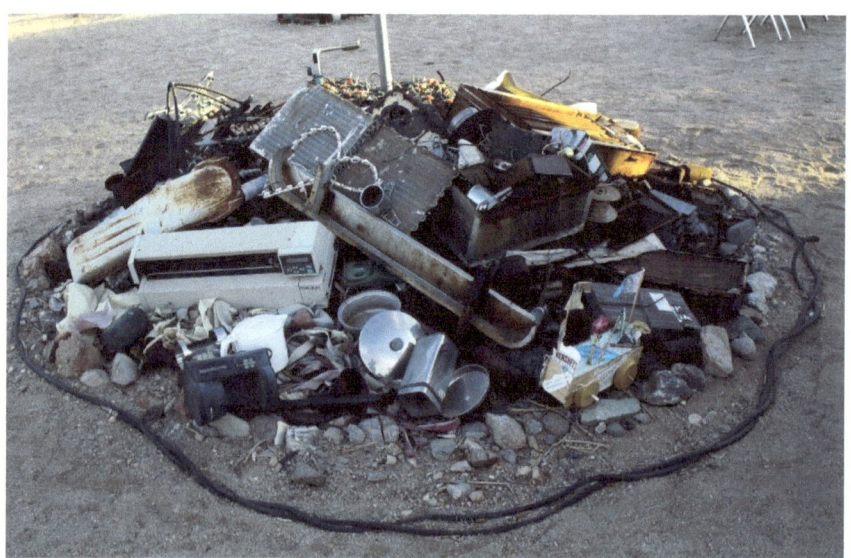

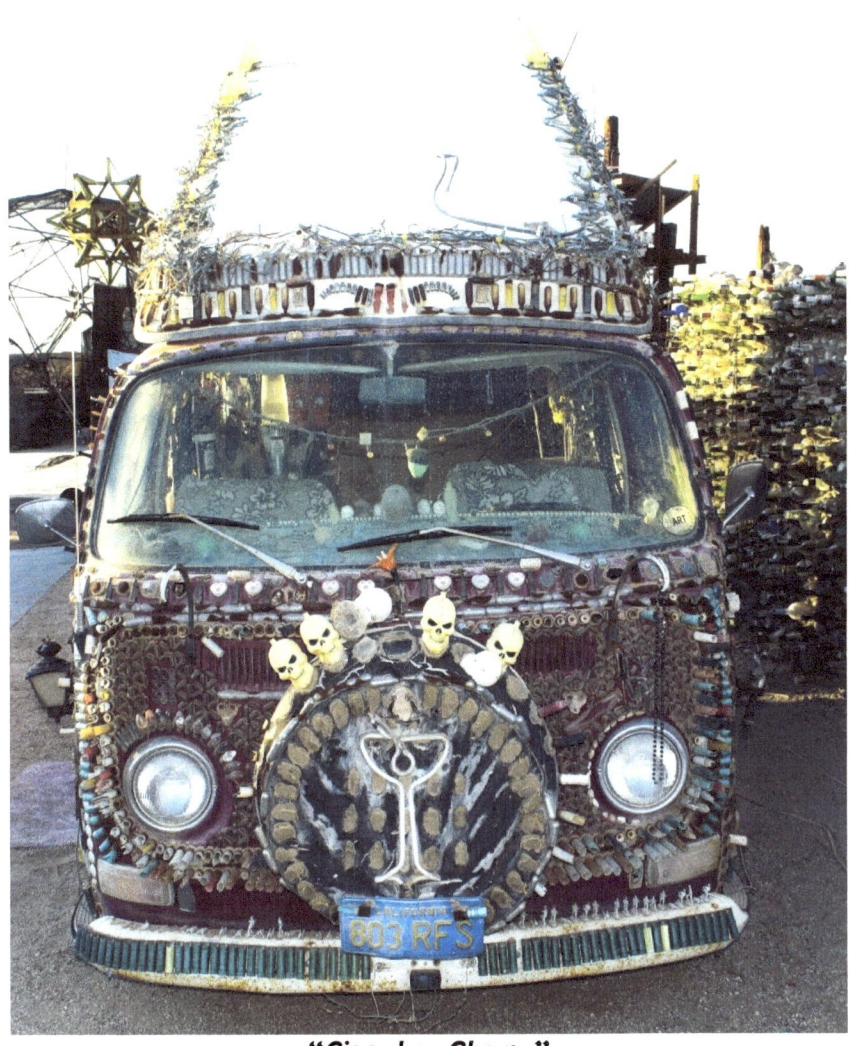

"Cinnabar Charm"

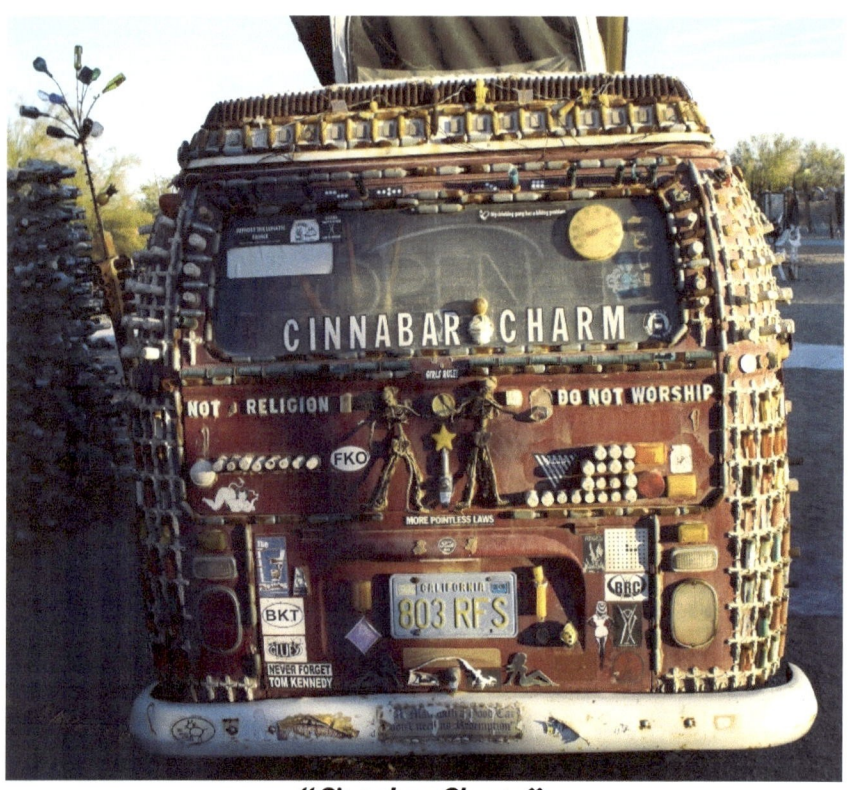

"Cinnabar Charm"

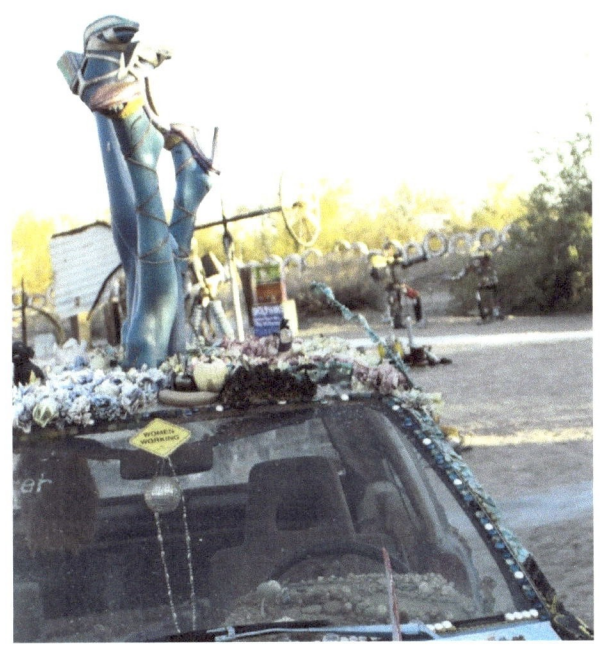

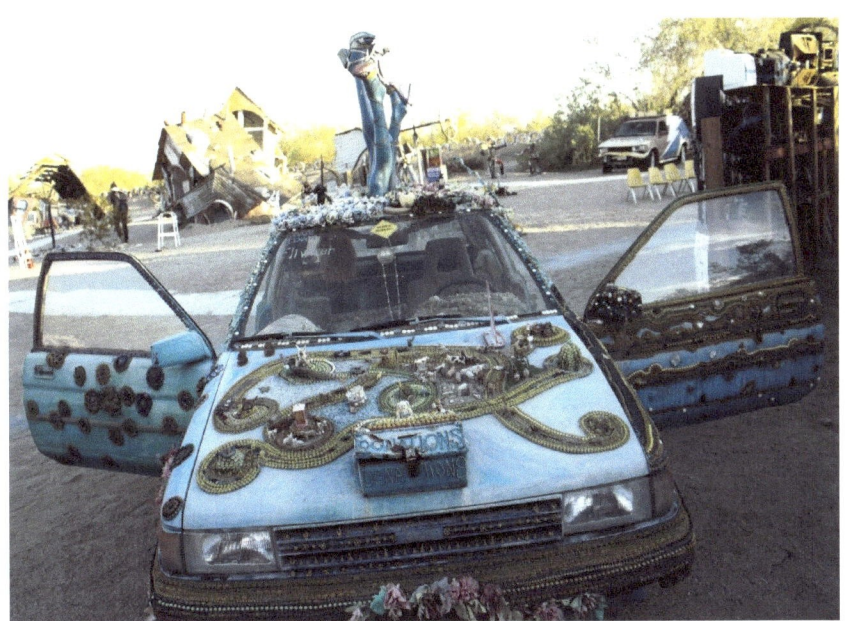

Working Women Sculpture

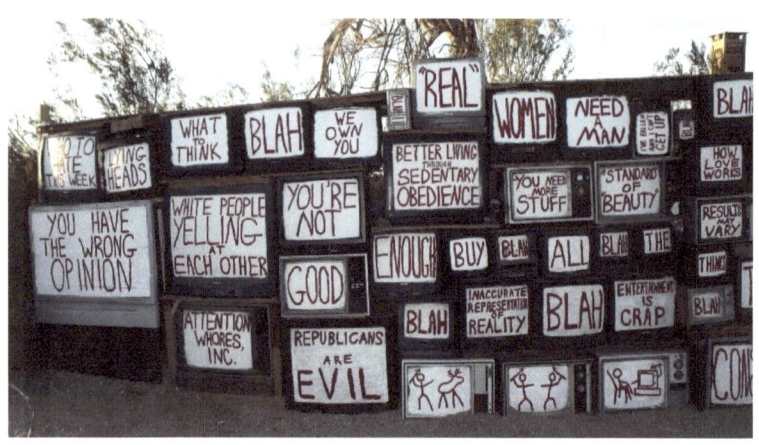

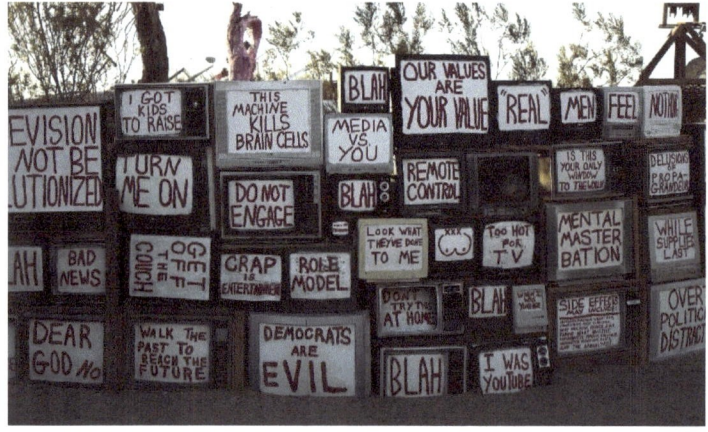

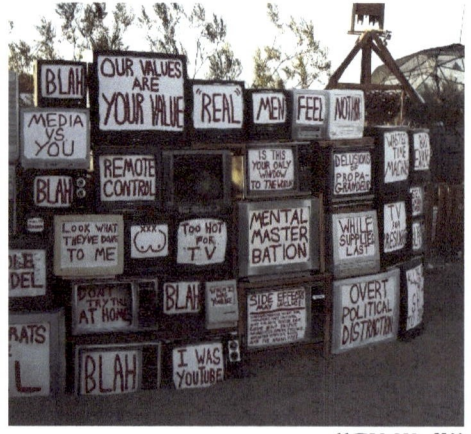

"TV Wall"

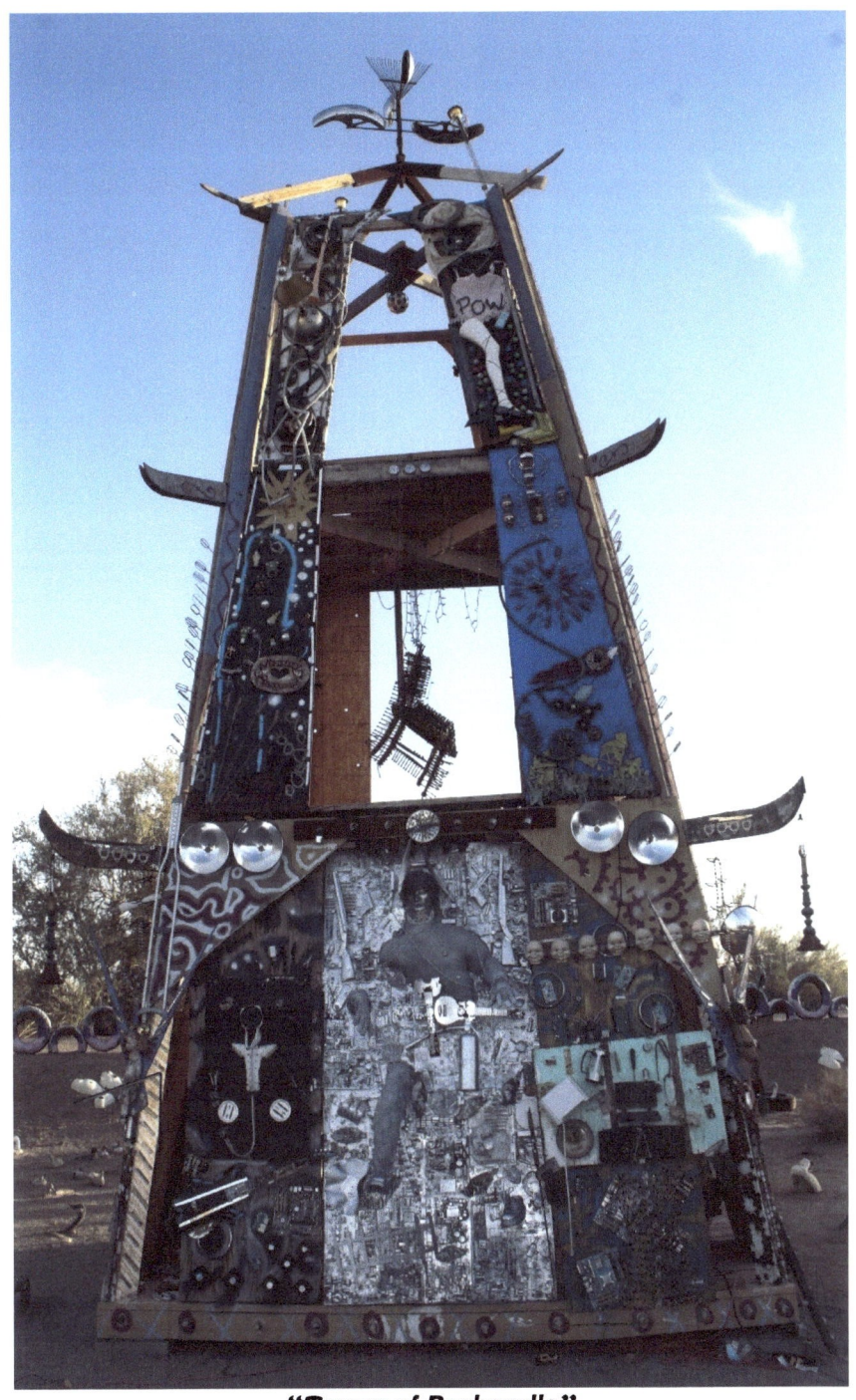

"Tower of Barbarella"

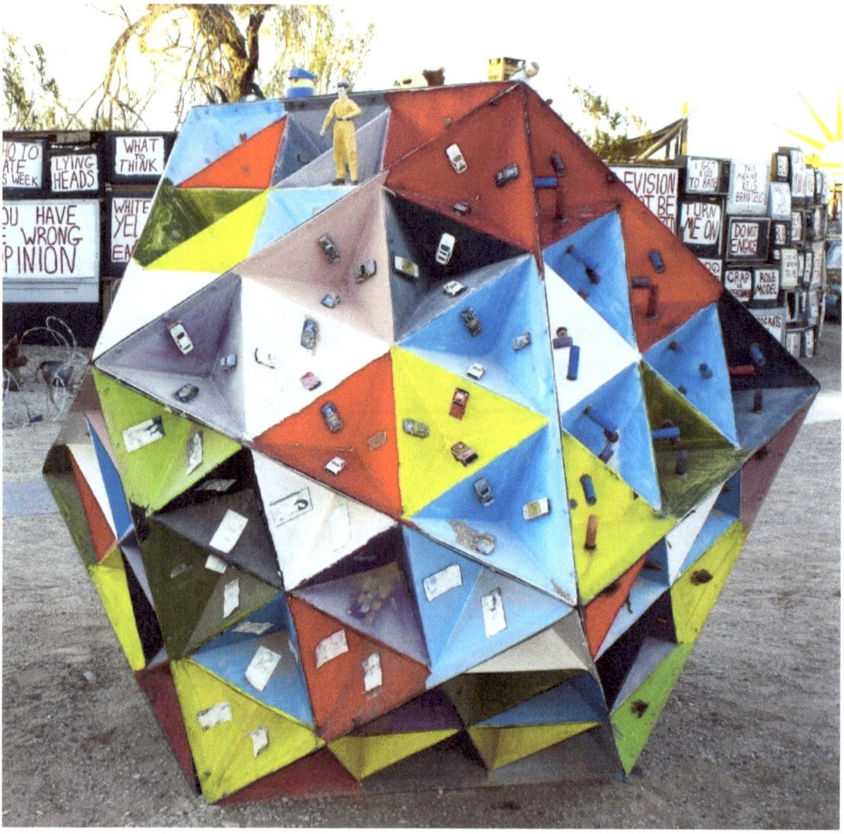

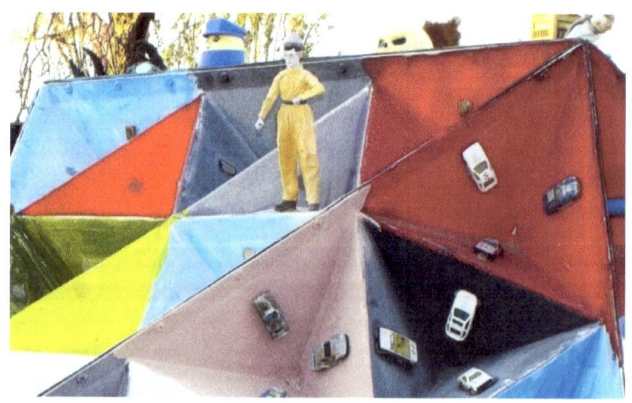

"Man's Vices"

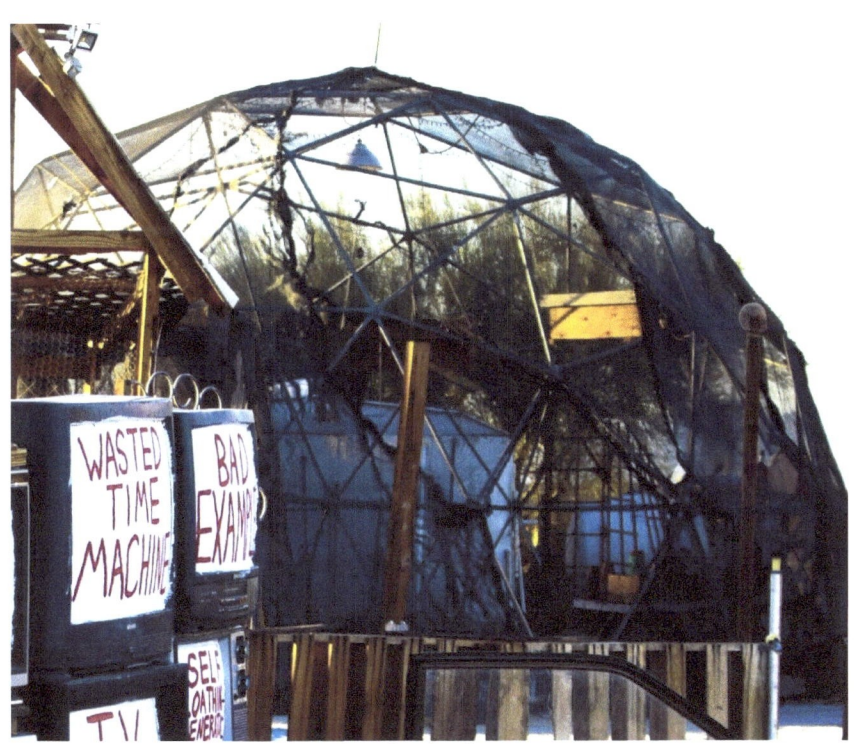

Geodesic dome

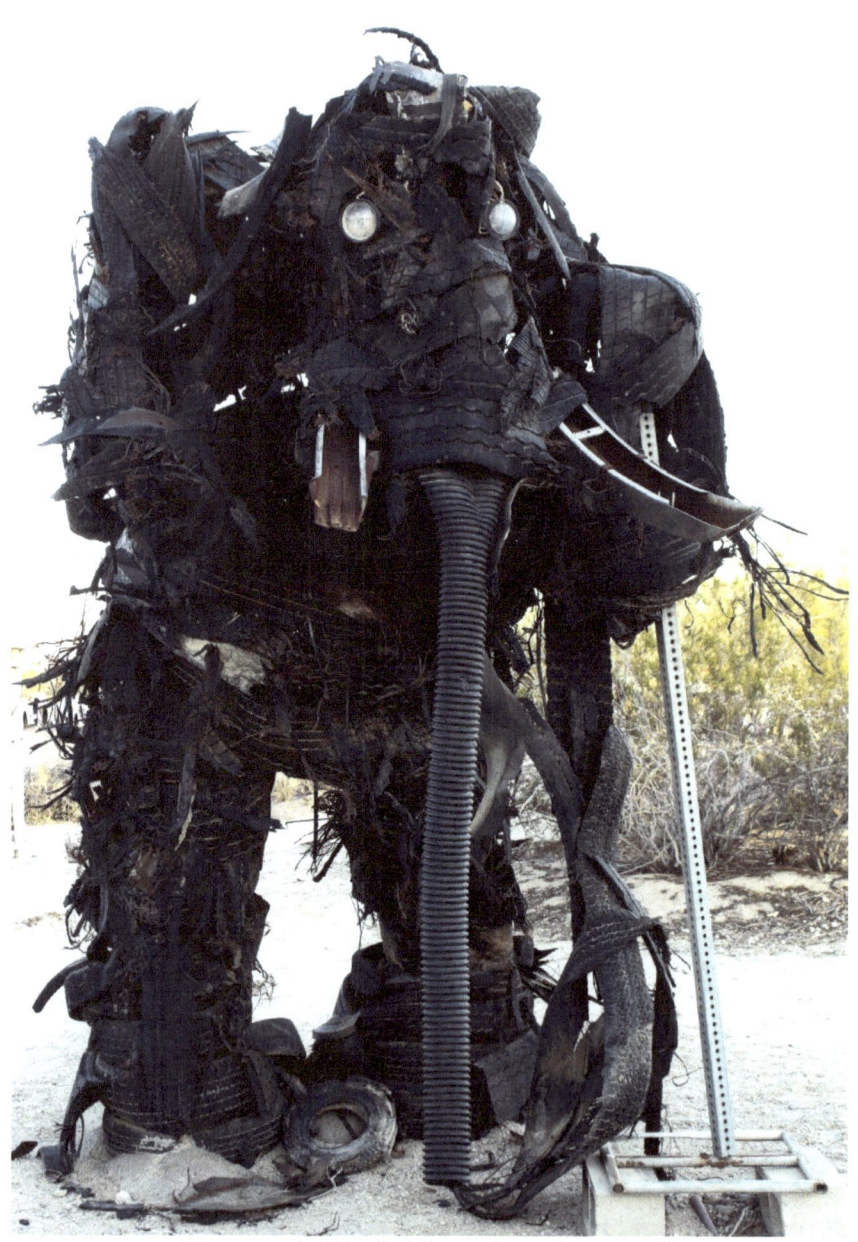

Mammoth "Definition of a grievance"

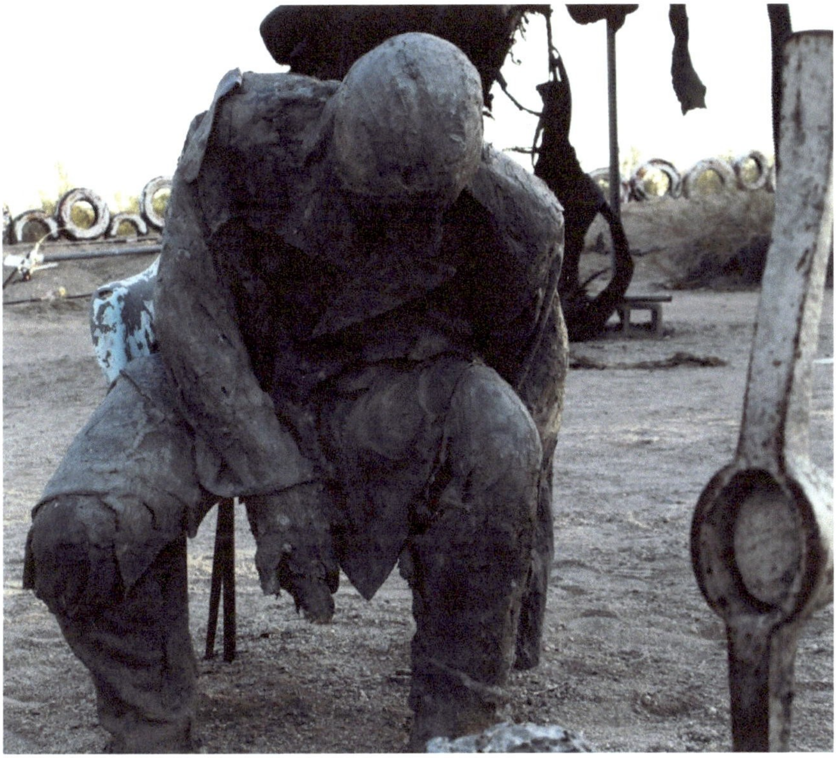

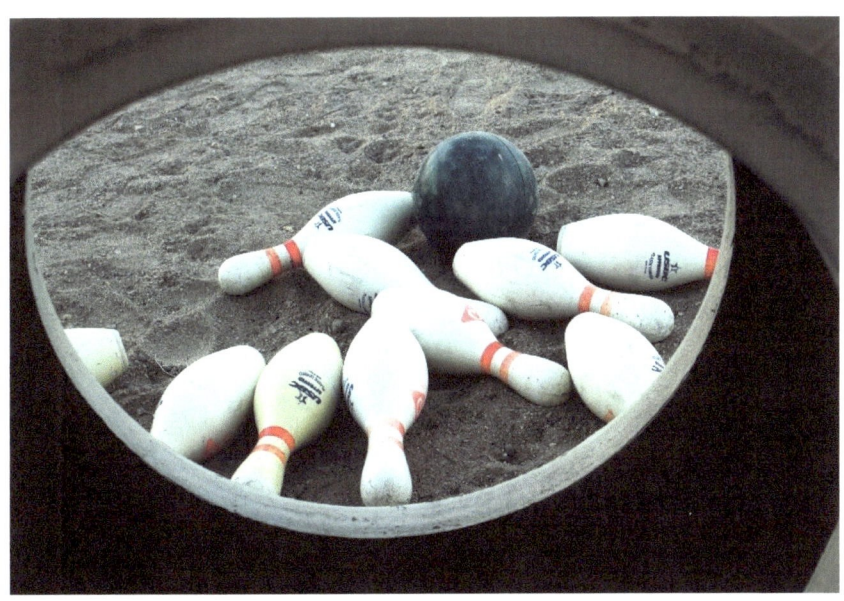

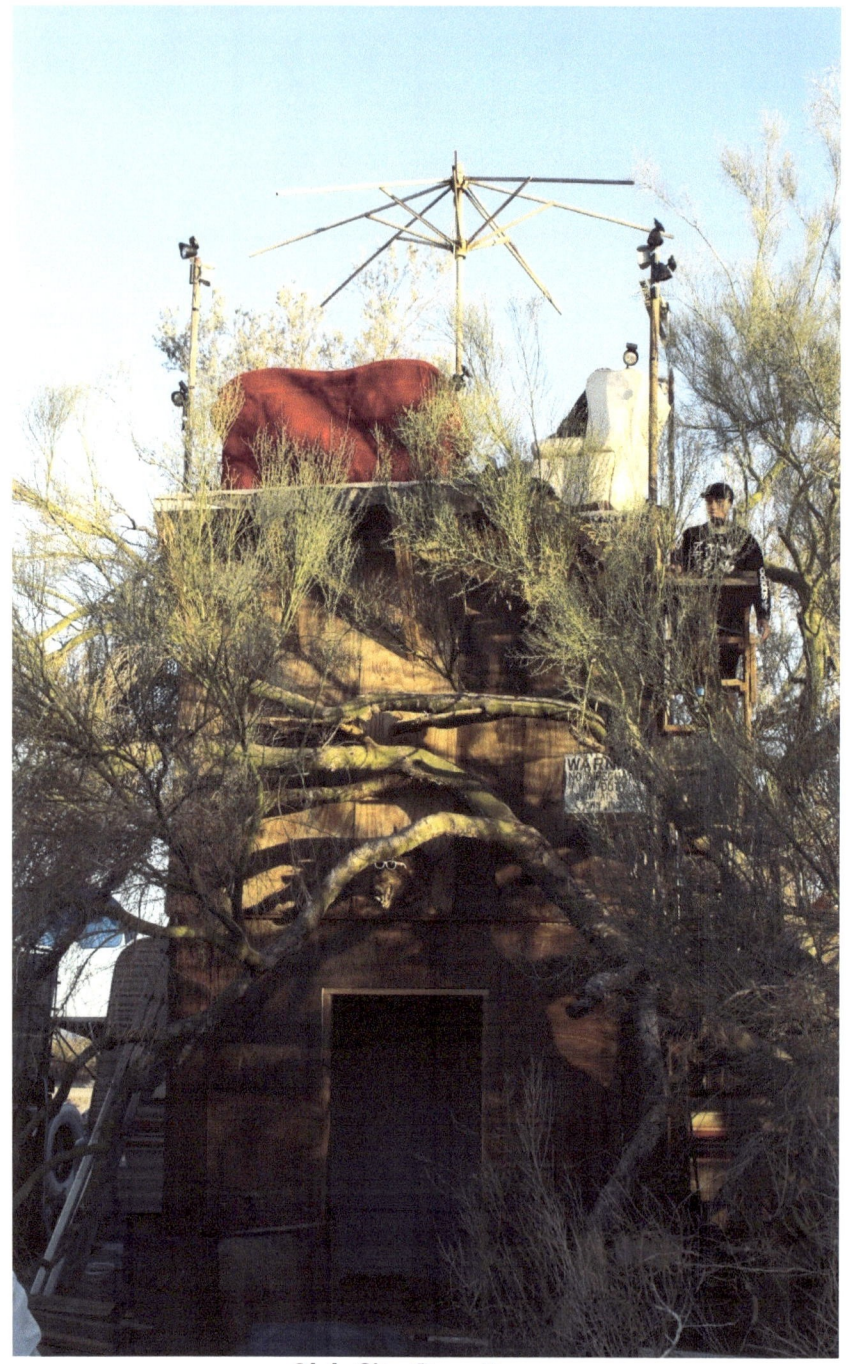

Slab City Tree House

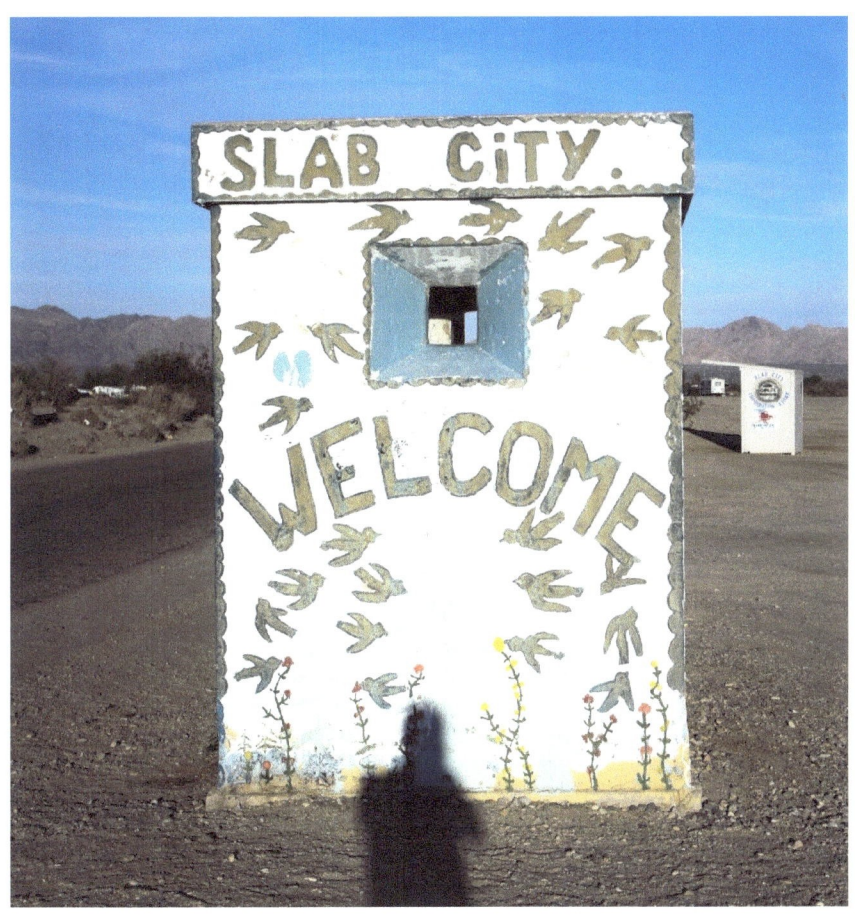

After leaving Slab City, we passed back by Salton Sea. I was able to take this last photo of the sunset over the sea, which was really great.

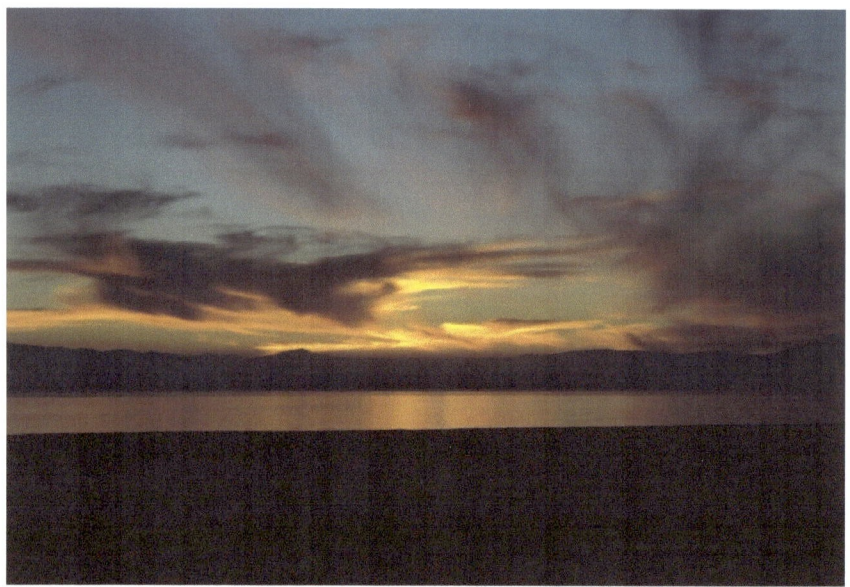

Sunset over the Salton Sea